The District Controller's View
THE WAVERLEY ROUTE
EDINBURGH - GALASHIELS - HAW[ICK]

The last of its type, LNER A1 Pacific 68 'Sir Visto' of Carlisle Canal backs onto the 10.05 Edinburgh to St Pancras in April 1948. If the engine looks a little dustier than the other Pacifics pulling out of Waverley, part of the reason is because 68 had been at work for some hours, having worked into Edinburgh with a Carlisle - Dundee goods followed by a Corstorphine - Edinburgh local. On reaching Carlisle 68 will work back to Edinburgh with the down 'Waverley' from St Pancras and return with a Dundee - Carlisle fast goods.

The first choice of route for most passengers to London was the East Coast main line whose 09.30 Edinburgh - Kings Cross 'Elizabethan' covered the 393 miles in seven and a half hours non-stop. To those for whom speed was a secondary consideration, the joint North British/Midland alternative via Hawick, Carlisle, Leeds and Nottingham - the Waverley Route - was by far the better option since in exchange for a journey three hours longer, one travelled through the very backbone of Britain and traversed two of the most scenic lines in the Kingdom.

Whether travelling to Carlisle or London, from a carriage window the line was spectacular and quite at odds with the impression given by the public timetable which a grudgingly listed a pair of London expresses together with a handful of stopping trains between Edinburgh, Hawick and Carlisle. The timetable reinforced the notion that the Waverley route was the least of the three mainline between Edinburgh and London and in doing so completely deflected attention from the hefty tonnage of goods that hourly blasted its way over Falahill and Whitrope.

One after another, goods trains with traffic for the Midland or North Western lines would pull out of Niddrie or one of the several goods yards in the Edinburgh area. The running time of around five hours for the one hundred miles to Canal Yard does not sound impressive - not that a 1950's lorry could do any better - but jokes about Waverley route trains travelling

as far vertically as they did horizontally had a germ of truth in them.

Goods trains from Edinburgh no sooner arrived on the route than they had to halt at Hardengreen Junction so that a J36 0-6-0 could buffer up to the brakevan and bank the train the ten miles - for which forty-three minutes were allowed - to Falahill summit.

An hour beyond Falahill trains would reach Hawick where crews would be exchanged with a northbound goods. At the same time another J36 would buffer onto the brakevan and assist in rear for the eleven miles and fifty-two minutes to Whitrope summit. Two hours were then granted for the remaining forty-five miles downhill to Carlisle where trains terminated in the Canal marshalling yard.

In the northbound direction goods trains were banked over the eight miles between Newcastleton and Riccarton Junction (or to Whitrope if the train engine was struggling). It will be seen that in the case of southbound trains, an appreciable proportion of the journey was accomplished with an engine at both ends of the train. Passenger trains had no such assistance and normally had to run the course with one engine only since banking was made

Thanks for assistance are due to: M. Bentley, H. Townley, G. Harrop, Iain Fraser, P. Webb, W.S.Sellar (Asst Controller, Edinburgh Rtd), A. Newman, W. Becket, D. Gill, A.D.Neale, J. Darby, M Nicholson and P. Dobson

difficult since the assisting engine had to couple to the rear of the train which meant an additional stop had to be made at the summits to uncouple the banker. Double-heading was similarly awkward since only a 4-4-0 was permitted to double-head an A3 or V2.

Whatever the operational peculiarities of the line, not even the most prosaic of its operators would deny it its sense of the romantic - a line where trains, less than half an hour out of the bustle of Edinburgh, were embraced by the loneliest wilderness and some of the most hostile elements that Britain could produce.

It was not Hadrian's Wall that kept the English and Scots apart so much as the Cheviot hills and the latter were indeed a formidable obstacle for trains as well as people. Clearly nature did not intend that movement between the Forth and the Solway should be easy and when a train eventually ran into the Citadel or Canal marshalling yard, its engine had indeed done a hard day's work. One might have wished the route had been given more appropriate engines since the A3's - designed for the level East Coast route - were not really suited to the mountainous profile of the line whilst the K3 2-6-0's which handled much of the goods traffic could have been better riding.

It would be a sad thing indeed if the fine detail of Waverley route operations were to fade with time and we hope that the following pages in which the line as it was in the 1950's is described may keep the memory alive for a few more years yet.

WORKING TIMETABLE (PASSENGER & GOODS) - EDINBURGH (WAV) to CARLISLE : 1953

m.ch / Station	1/in	625	560	569	560	509	560	119	522	227	G	61	78	577	523	7	553	229	229	553	228	651	344	230
Train		22.05	01.00	20.20	01.00	00.55	01.00							22.25			23.05				23.05	10.43	00.30	07.56
From		Dundee	Niddrie	A'deen	Niddrie	I'kthing	Niddrie			News	EBV			A'deen			D'dee				D'dee	L'holm	D'dee	E'bro
Class		C	J	C	J	C	J	LE	F	News	EBV	B	B	C	H	LE	E	LE	B	E	E	E	E	B
Engine		A3	J35	K3	J35	K3	J35	D30	D49	B1		D30	D30	K3	J37	J39	A3	J39	B1	A3	A3	K3	V1	B1
0.00 EDINBURGH (WAV)			00/38							04.10							05/43				06.35			08.35
3.00 Portobello	-166		00/44						02.25	04/16							05/52				06.45			08.41
4.33 Niddrie S. Jcn	+112	00/48	01/04	01/48					02/34	04/18				04/53	05/16		05/59				06/48	07/33		08/44
6.19 Millerhill Jcn	+259																							
7.76 Eskbank	+196																				06.54			08.50
8.21 Hardengreen Jcn	+226	00.56	01.18	01.56		02.31			02.46					05.01			06.09				07.43			
8.21 Hardengreen Jcn			01B01	01B25	02B02		02B36		03B00	04/24				05B08	05/27		06B15				06/55	07B48		08/51
9.56 Newtongrange	+79																							08.55
12.01 Gorebridge	+83																				07.05			09.02
12.61 Fushiebridge	+70																							
16.01 Tynehead	+70																				07.15			
17.76 Falahill	+73		01/37	02.15	02/38	02.45	03/12		03/48	04/44				05/44	06/17		06/58				07/21	08/31		09/17
19.09 Heriot	-192																				07.23			09.20
22.45 Fountainhall	-122																				07.29			09.27
26.52 Stow	-224																				07.37			09.34
29.62 Bowland	-169																				07.44			
32.40 Kilknowe Jcn	-116																					09/38		
33.43 GALASHIELS	-115			03.22					04.20	05.03											07.51	09/40		09.47
33.43 GALASHIELS			01/57	02/58		(03.40)	03/32	03.40	04.30	05.11	05.15			06/04	06/49		07/24				07.54	08/57		09.49
37.17 Melrose	-785									05.20											08.02			09.56
40.45 ST BOSWELLS JCN	+1812	02.09					04.02		04.51		05.35			07.08							08.09			10.02
40.45 ST BOSWELLS JCN		02.25		03.08		03.42			05.01	05.31				06.14	07.18		07.37				08.13	09/10		10.04
41.72 Charlesfield	+348																				08.19			
45.13 Belses	+573																				08.27			10.12
48.43 Hassendean	+1413																				08.35			10.19
52.67 HAWICK	-260			03.28			04.02		05.33	05.48				06.35	07.52		08.03				08.44	09.36		10.26
52.67 HAWICK			02/46	03B55		04B35						06.15		07B05							08.53	09B05		10B20
55.27 Stobs Camp	+99																							
56.56 Stobs	+79											06.24									09.02			
59.67 Shankend	+98											06.32									09.10			
63.55 Whitrope Summit	+81		03/18	04/30		05/10	05.15					06/42		07/40							09.21	10/00		11/15
65.68 RICCARTON JCN	-91											06.47									09.24			
65.68 RICCARTON JCN			03/21	04/33		05/13	05/20					06.49		07.12	07/43						09.25	10/03		11/18
69.32 Steele Road	-75											(to									09.31			
73.77 Newcastleton	-85											N'cstle)		07.24							09.39			
73.77 Newcastleton			03/31	04/43		05/23	05/35							07.30	07/53						09.40	10/17		11/32
77.04 Kershope Foot	-605													07.39							09.47			
81.46 Penton	+3299													07.46							09.56			
84.12 Riddings Jcn	-109																	09.00			10.03		11.00	
88.49 LONGTOWN JCN	-261		03/50	05/04		05/42	06.00							07.55	08/12			09/08			10.13	10/42	11.09	11/57
90.52 Fauldmoor	-556																							
91.46 Lyneside	+558																							
93.64 Harker	+316															08.30								
94.18 Parkhouse	-3153													08.02							10.20		11/15	
95.05 Brunthill	-552		03/50	05/12			05/50								08/20	09/20				08/35	10.52	10/56	12/07	
96.68 Canal Jcn	-685		04/01	05/16			05/53					08.08			08/23	09/23				08/38	10/25	10.56	11/20	12/11
97.18 Canal Yard			04.04	05.19			05.56								08.26	09.25				08.40	10.59		12.14	
98.15 CARLISLE	+455											08.12									10.29	11.24		
Destination																								
Due																								

WORKING TIMETABLE (PASSENGER & GOODS) - CARLISLE to EDINBURGH (WAV) : 1953

m.ch / Station	1/in	528	768	767	528	540	618	253	567	185	216	217	567	221	555	656	656	958	119	558	558	13	13	7
Train					00.10				21.05			04.20				06.05				09.00		07.00		
From					Canal				St. P			Canal				Canal				Hawick		Canal		
Class		E	C	C	E	K	V2	Pcls	E	A	V1	B	B	B	K	D	B	D30	D	E	K	K	B	B
Engine		A3	A3	V2	A3	J36	V2	A4	K3	A3	V1	D49	K3	B1	J39	B1	B1	J67	D30	J37	J37	J39	J39	J39
0.00 CARLISLE								04.08		05.10														
(0.77) Canal Yard		00.10	01.10	01.30			02.15		04.20					05.25		06.05						07.00		07.30
1.27 Canal Jcn	-455	00/12	01/12	01/32			02/17	04/12	04/22	05/14				05/28		06/07						07/02		07/34
3.10 Brunthill	+685	00/15	01/15	01/35			02/20		04/25					05/31		06/10								
3.77 Parkhouse	+552																							07/43
4.31 Harker	+3153																							07/45
9.46 LONGTOWN JCN	-1024	00/26	01/24	01/44			02/31	04/21	04/36	05/23				05/51		06/20						07/20	07/30	
14.03 Riddings Jcn	+261	00/35	01/31	01/51			02/40		04/45					06/07		06/28								
16.49 Penton	+109													(to										
21.11 Kershope Foot	-3299	00.57					03.02			05.41				L'holm) 06.48									08.05	
24.18 Newcastleton	+605								05.07	05.41						06.48				08.00				
24.18 Newcastleton			01B04	01/48			02/08	04/38		05.42						06B55				08.00				
28.63 Steele Road	+85																			08.11				
32.27 RICCARTON JCN	+75								05.28											08.19				
32.27 RICCARTON JCN			01/42	02/09	02/29			03/47	04/55	(06.12)		06/01		06.12		07/28				08.20				
34.40 Whitrope Summit	+91		01/50	02/15	02/35			03/55	05/00			06/06		06/23		07/35				08/27				
38.28 Shankend	-81																			08.33				
41.39 Stobs	-98																			08.39				
42.68 Stobs Camp	-79	02.10			03.06											07.55	08.07							
45.28 HAWICK	-99		02/34	02/54	03/17		04/22	05.16		06.22			06.50			08.17				08.46				
45.28 HAWICK			02.45	03.05	03.50		04.42	05.29		06.27		06.44	07.25	08.07		08.45				09.00				
49.52 Hassendean	+260													08.14										
53.02 Belses	-1413													08.21										
56.23 Charlesfield	-573											07.01												
57.50 ST BOSWELLS JCN	-348							05.45		06.43		07.06		08.28						09.20				
57.50 ST BOSWELLS JCN			03/06	03/26	04/17	04.50	05/09	05.50		06.47		07.08	07/52	08.30		09/09				09.40				
60.78 Melrose	-1812							05.58		06.54		07.15		08.37										
64.52 GALASHIELS	+785					05.11		06.04		07.00		07.21		08.43										
64.52 GALASHIELS			03/16	03/36	04/31		05/23	06.09		07.05	07/13	07.23		08.44	08/06	09/21		09.26		09/57				
65.55 Kilknowe Jcn	+115									07/15														
68.33 Bowland	+116																							
71.43 Stow	+169											07.38		08.57										
75.50 Fountainhall	+224											07.47		09.05					10.06					
79.06 Heriot	+122											07.54							(To					
80.19 Falahill	+192		03/46	04/06	05/16		06/08	06/33		07/28				08/51	09/14		10/01		Lauder)	10.44	10.55			
82.14 Tynehead	-73											08.01												
85.34 Fushiebridge	-70																							
86.14 Gorebridge	-70											08.09												
88.38 Newtongrange	-83											08.14												
89.74 Hardengreen Jcn	-79		04/01	04/21	05/41		06/33	06/47		07/41		08/17	09/16	09/27		10/21					11.25			
90.19 Eskbank	-226											08.19												
91.76 Millerhill Jcn	-196											08.23					10/28							
93.62 Niddrie S. Jcn	-259		04/07	04/27	05/59		06/41	06/53		07/46		08/27	09/24	09/32										
95.15 Portobello	-112							06.56		07.48		08.31	09/29	09/34										
98.15 EDINBURGH (WAV)	+166							07.02		07.54		08.37		09.40										
Destination			Dundee	Perth	Niddrie		Meadows			E'bro						A'deen								
Due			07.30	07.20	05.54		06.55			08.49						18.58								

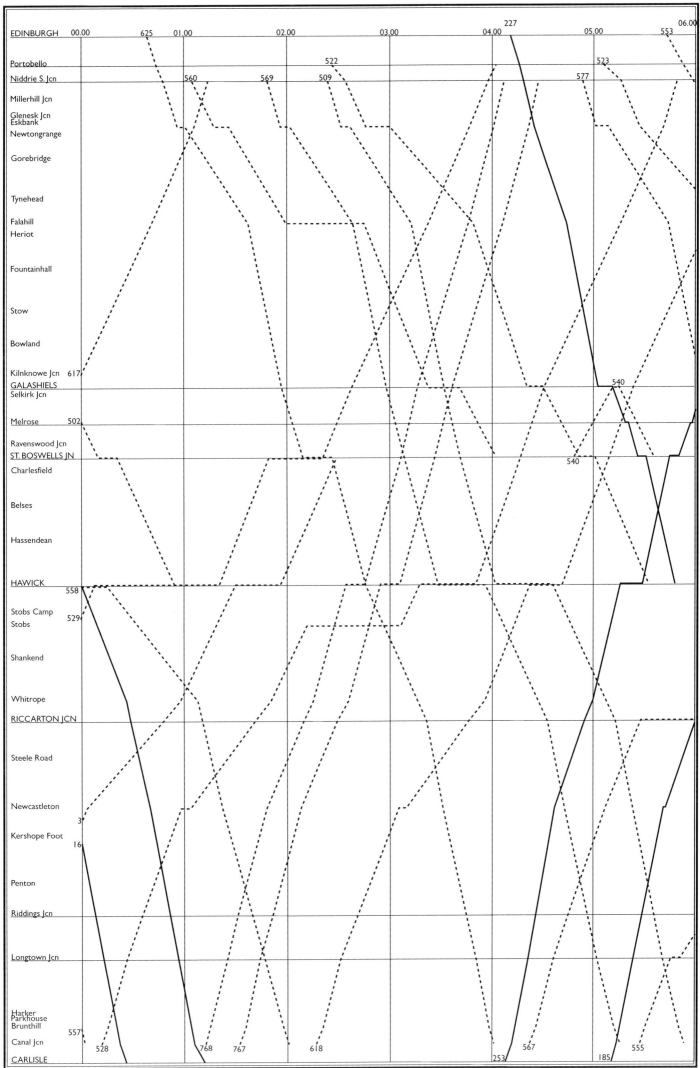

EDINBURGH 00.00 625 01.00 02.00 03.00 227 04.00 05.00 553 06.00

Portobello 522 523
Niddrie S. Jcn 560 569 509 577
Millerhill Jcn
Glenesk Jcn
Eskbank
Newtongrange

Gorebridge

Tynehead

Falahill
Heriot

Fountainhall

Stow

Bowland

Kilknowe Jcn 617
GALASHIELS 540
Selkirk Jcn

Melrose 502

Ravenswood Jcn
ST. BOSWELLS JN 540
Charlesfield

Belses

Hassendean

HAWICK 558
Stobs Camp 529
Stobs

Shankend

Whitrope

RICCARTON JCN

Steele Road

Newcastleton 3

Kershope Foot 16

Penton

Riddings Jcn

Longtown Jcn

Harker
Parkhouse
Brunthill
Canal Jcn 557
CARLISLE 528 768 767 618 253 567 185 555

WORKING TIMETABLE (PASSENGER & GOODS) - EDINBURGH (WAV) to CARLISLE : 1953

m.ch / Station	1 in																					
Train		09.00	09.00	09.00	09.00		09.00	09.00	09.20	09.00	11.45	11.45	11.45	11.45		09.00	01.00		11.45	11.45	10.30	11.45
From		H'green	H'green	H'green	H'green	A	H'green	H'green	P'bles	H'green	Hawick	Hawick	Hawick	Hawick	E	H'green	A'deen	A	Hawick	Hawick	P'bello	Hawick
Class		K	K	K	K	A	K	K	J36	K	J39	J39	J39	J39	E	K3	E	A	J39	J39	K3	J39
Engine	J35	J35	J35	J35	J35	A3	J35	J35	J36	J35	J39	J39	J39	J39	K3	J35	K3	A3	J39	J39	K3	J39
Rep No.	1 in	524	524	524	524	132	524	524	520	524	108	108	108	108	525	524	539	232	108	108	525	108
0.00 EDINBURGH (WAV)						10.05												12.05				
3.00 Portobello	-166					10/11												12/11			10.30	
4.33 Niddrie S. Jcn	+112					10/13											11/04	12/13			10/40	
6.19 Millerhill Jcn	+259																					
7.76 Eskbank	+196																					
8.21 Hardengreen Jcn	+226																11.15				10.50	
8.21 Hardengreen Jcn		09.00				10/18											11B20	12/18			10B56	
9.56 Newtongrange	+79																					
12.01 Gorebridge	+83	09.10	09.20																			
12.61 Fushiebridge	+70		09.25	09.35																		
16.01 Tynehead	+70			09.45	10.05																	
17.76 Falahill	+73				10.15	10/38	10.25									11/39	12/03	12/37				
19.09 Heriot	-192						10.30	10.40														
22.45 Fountainhall	-122							10.55		11.05												
26.52 Stow	-224									11.20												
29.62 Bowland	-169									11.40											11.50	
32.40 Kilknowe Jcn	-116								11/35													
33.43 GALASHIELS	-115					10.57			11.40									12.55			12.10	
33.43 GALASHIELS						11.00											12.29	12.57			12.05	
37.17 Melrose	-785					11.08												13.04				
40.45 ST BOSWELLS JCN	+1812					11.14											12.44	13.10				
40.45 ST BOSWELLS JCN						11.18											(13.23)	13.15			12.18	
41.72 Charlesfield	+348																					
45.13 Belses	+573																					
48.43 Hassendean	+1413																					
52.67 HAWICK	-260					11.33												13.30			12.44	
52.67 HAWICK						11.37					11.45							13.33				13B42
55.27 Stobs Camp	+99																					
56.56 Stobs	+79										12.00	12.10										
59.67 Shankend	+98											12.20	12.30									
63.55 Whitrope Summit	+81					12/03							12/45					13/57				14/37
65.68 RICCARTON JCN	-91												12.50					14.00				
65.68 RICCARTON JCN						12/06								13.00				14.01				14/40
69.32 Steele Road	-75													13.15	13.25							
73.77 Newcastleton	-85														13.40			14.13				
73.77 Newcastleton						12/16								13.50				14.14	14.20			14/54
77.04 Kershope Foot	-605													14.00					14.35	14.45		
81.46 Penton	+3299																		14.45	14.55		15.20
84.12 Riddings Jcn	-109																			14.55		15.20
88.49 LONGTOWN JCN	-261					12/33												14.32		15/19		15.35
90.52 Fauldmoor	-556																					
91.46 Lyneside	+558																					
93.64 Harker	+316																					
94.18 Parkhouse	-3153																					
95.05 Brunthill	-552																			15/29		
96.68 Canal Jcn	-685					12/44												14.41		15/33		
97.18 Canal Yard																				15.39		
98.15 CARLISLE	+455					12.48												14.45				
Destination						St P.																
Due						20.45																

WORKING TIMETABLE (PASSENGER & GOODS) - CARLISLE to EDINBURGH (WAV) : 1953

m.ch / Station	1 in																							
Train		07.00		09.00				07.00	07.00	07.00	08.00							13.00		13.00		11.35	13.00	
From		Canal		Hawick				Canal	Canal	Canal	Canal							G'shiels		G'shiels		Hawick	G'shiels	
Class		K	V1	D	E	B	ECS	K	K	K	B	D	B	J36	J36	H	K	K	D30	K	F	B	H	K
Engine	1 in	J39	V1	K3	J37	9	J39	J39	J39	J39	A3	K3	B1	J36	J36	J37	K3	J35	D30	J35	J37	V1	J37	J35
Rep No.		13	222	503	558	9	229	13	13	13	227	503	228	23	574	521	569	569	21	569	557	236	521	569
0.00 CARLISLE						08.10					09.05													
(0.77) Canal Yard				08.00														09.45						
1.27 Canal Jcn	-455			08/02		08/14					09/09							09/48						
3.10 Brunthill	+685			08/05																				
3.77 Parkhouse	+552					08.20																		
4.31 Harker	+3153					08.24	08.30																	
9.46 LONGTOWN JCN	-1024			08/15							09.23							10.28						
14.03 Riddings Jcn	+261			08/23			08.45				09.33													
16.49 Penton	+109										09.39													
21.11 Kershope Foot	-3299										09.48													
24.18 Newcastleton	+605			08.45							09.55													
24.18 Newcastleton			08.15	08.50							09.56													
28.63 Steele Road	+85										10.07													
32.27 RICCARTON JCN	+75		08.55								10.16													
32.27 RICCARTON JCN				09/23				09.30			10.19													
34.40 Whitrope Summit	+91			09/30							10/25													
38.28 Shankend	-81							09.45	09.55		10.32													
41.39 Stobs	-98								10.05	10.15	10.39													
42.68 Stobs Camp	-79																							
45.28 HAWICK	-99			09.54						10.30	10.46													
45.28 HAWICK				10.15							10.52		11.11			11.35								
49.52 Hassendean	+260												11.23											
53.02 Belses	-1413																							
56.23 Charlesfield	-573																							
57.50 ST BOSWELLS JCN	-348										11.09	11.30				12.10								
57.50 ST BOSWELLS JCN											11.13	11.35	12.05			12.20								
60.78 Melrose	-1812										11.20	11.42	12.18											
64.52 GALASHIELS	+785										11.27	11.49				12.41								
64.52 GALASHIELS				10.16	10/50						11.31	11.55				12.15	12.50	13.00						
65.55 Kilknowe Jcn	+115			10/18									12/20											
68.33 Bowland	+116																13.15	13.25						
71.43 Stow	+169												12.11				13.35							
75.50 Fountainhall	+224												12.20				14.00							
79.06 Heriot	+122												12.28				14.10							
80.19 Falahill	+192			11.30							11/54	12.02	12/30				13.50	14.00					14.20	
82.14 Tynehead	-73																							
85.34 Fushiebridge	-70																							
86.14 Gorebridge	-70												12.44							14.06				
88.38 Newtongrange	-83																			14.11				
89.74 Hardengreen Jcn	-79				11.40						12/07	12/25	12.52					14.00		14/13		14.37		
90.19 Eskbank	-226												12.54							14.15				
91.76 Millerhill Jcn	-196				11/51																			
93.62 Niddrie S. Jcn	-259				11/51						12/12	12/32	13/02							14/12		14/21		
95.15 Portobello	-112				11.58						12.14		13.05									14.24		
98.15 EDINBURGH (WAV)	+166										12.20		13.11									14.30		
Destination				E'bro							Perth		P'bles					T'ton Jn						
Due				11.48							17.26		13.55					17.10						

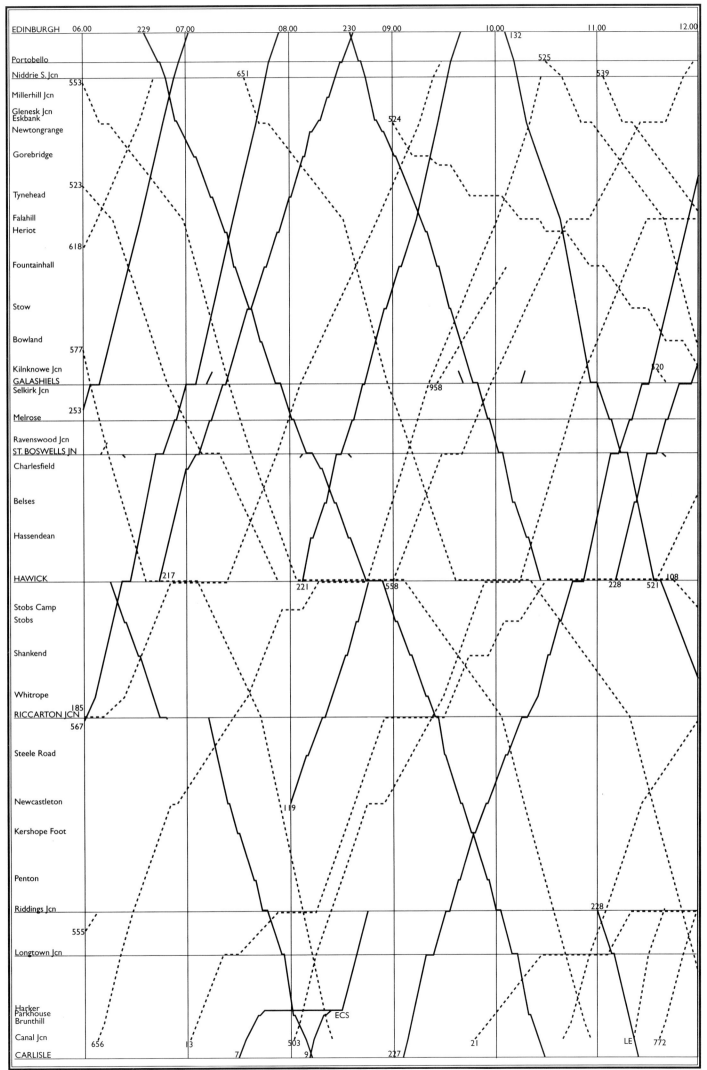

EDINBURGH   06.00   229   07.00   08.00   230   09.00   10.00   132   11.00   12.00
Portobello   525
Niddrie S. Jcn   651   539
553
Millerhill Jcn
Glenesk Jcn
Eskbank   524
Newtongrange

Gorebridge

523
Tynehead

Falahill
Heriot
618
Fountainhall

Stow

Bowland
577
Kilnknowe Jcn   520
GALASHIELS
Selkirk Jcn   958
253
Melrose

Ravenswood Jcn
ST. BOSWELLS JN
Charlesfield

Belses

Hassendean

HAWICK   217   221   558   228   521   108
Stobs Camp
Stobs

Shankend

Whitrope
185
RICCARTON JCN
567

Steele Road

Newcastleton   119

Kershope Foot

Penton

Riddings Jcn   228
555
Longtown Jcn

Harker
Parkhouse   ECS
Brunthill
Canal Jcn   656   13   7   503   9   227   21   LE   772
CARLISLE

5

Train			01.00	11.45	12.15		15.30	11.45	11.45					13.18	13.30	13.30	13.30	14.25	18.24	14.55		14.55			16.35
From			A'deen	Hawick	Lauder		L'holm	Hawick	Hawick					E'bro	Niddrie	Niddrie	Niddrie	B'bank	L'holm	Niddrie		Niddrie			Niddrie
Class			E	K	K	K	B	K	K	B	H	B	B	B	E	B	B	E	H	B	H	B	H	K	E
Engine			K3	J39	J36	J67	LM4	J39	J39	V1	J39	J39	V1	K3	A3	D30	K3	J39	LM4	K3	D30	K3	B1	J36	K3
m.ch	1/in	**Rep No.**	539	108	2	958	444	108	108	233	70	74	348	500	235	177	500	521	446	537	140	537	237	586	517
0.00		**EDINBURGH (WAV)**								13.03					14,33							16.10			
3.00	-166	Portobello								13.11					14,39							16.16			
4.33	+112	Niddrie S. Jcn								13.14				13.33	14,41			14.59				16.19			16/38
6.19	+259	Millerhill Jcn								13.18												16.22			
7.76	+196	Eskbank								13.23												16.27			
8.21	+226	Hardengreen Jcn																							16.48
8.21		Hardengreen Jcn								13.24				13.43	14.46			15B17				16.28			16B53
9.56	+79	Newtongrange								13.28												16.32			
12.01	+83	Gorebridge								13.34												16.39			
12.61	+70	Fushiebridge																							
16.01	+70	Tynehead																				16.49			
17.76	+73	Falahill												14.32	15.06			16.10				16.56			17.36
19.09	-192	Heriot																				16.59			
22.45	-122	Fountainhall			13.15																				
26.52	-224	Stow													15.18							17.10			
29.62	-169	Bowland																							
32.40	-116	Kilknowe Jcn								14/52															
33.43	-115	**GALASHIELS**			13.40					14.54					15.28							17.21			
33.43		**GALASHIELS**								14/58					15.32			16/42				17.24		17.45	18/02
37.17	-785	Melrose		13.30											15.40							17.31			
40.45	+1812	**ST BOSWELLS JCN**		13.44											15.46							17.37			18.08
40.45		**ST BOSWELLS JCN**	13.23							15.18					15.51						17.15	17.41			18/15
41.72	+348	Charlesfield																			17.21	17.47			
45.13	+573	Belses																			17.28	17.54			
48.43	+1413	Hassendean																			17.35	18.01			
52.67	-260	**HAWICK**	13.52							15.47					16.06						17.42	18.08			18.41
52.67		**HAWICK**	14B10										(16.45)		16.14	16.32	16B45						(18.05)	18B05	
55.27	+99	Stobs Camp																							
56.56	+79	Stobs													16.23	16.41									
59.67	+98	Shankend													16.31	16.49									
63.55	+81	Whitrope Summit	15/05												16/41	17/00			17/40						
65.68	-91	**RICCARTON JCN**													16.44	17.01									
65.68		**RICCARTON JCN**	15/08												16.45	17.03	17/43								19/13
69.32	-75	Steele Road													16.51	(To									
73.77	-85	Newcastleton													16.58	N'ctle)									
73.77		Newcastleton	15/22													16.59	17/57								19/32
77.04	-605	Kershope Foot														17.05									
81.46	+3299	Penton														17.14									
84.12	-109	Riddings Jcn					15.50									17.22			18.44						19/56
88.49	-261	**LONGTOWN JCN**	15/47			15.50	15/57									17.32	18/22	18.42	18.55						20/05
90.52	-556	Fauldmoor														17.35									
91.46	+558	Lyneside				16.00		16.10																	
93.64	+316	Harker					16.04	16.15	16.20				17.30						19.10						
94.18	-3153	Parkhouse					16.07						17.34						19.14						
95.05	-552	Brunthill	15/57						16.50								18/32	18/59							20/19
96.68	-685	Canal Jcn	16/01				16/12	16/30	17/10				17/40			17/48	18/36	19.03	19/19						20/23
97.18		Canal Yard	16.04					16.35	17.15								18/39	19/07							20.26
98.15	+455	**CARLISLE**					16.16						17.44			17.52			19.23						
		Destination Due																							

			b1	b2	b3	b4	b5	b6	b7	b8	b9	b10	b11	b12	b13	b14	b15	b16	b17	b18	b19	b20	b21	b22	b23
Train			13.00	11.35		13.00	09.45	11.35	11.45	13.00	13.00	11.35	09.45		09.45	11.20	13.00	11.35					13.35		
From			G'shiels	Hawick		G'shiels	Canal		Canal	G'shiels	G'shiels	Canal	Canal		Canal	Ncle	G'shiels	Canal					Canal		
Class			K	H	E	K	K	Light	K	K	K	E	K	H	K	B	A	K	E	B	B	E	E	E	H
Engine			J35	J37	K3	J35	D30	LM4	J35	J35	K3	D30	J39	D30	D30	A3	J35	K3	V1	D30	K3	K3	B1	K3	K3
m.ch	1/in	**Rep No.**	569	521	600	569	21	295	569	569	772	21	576	21	4862	244	569	772	246	117	518	518	594	250	504
0.00		**CARLISLE**														13.26									15.37
(0.77)		Canal Yard			10.40			11.21	11.35		12.15							13.35				14.35		16.00	
1.27	-455	Canal Jcn			10/42						12/18					13/30		13/37				14/37	15/41	16/03	
3.10	+685	Brunthill			10/45						12/21					13/40						14/40		16/06	
3.77	+552	Parkhouse																							
4.31	+3153	Harker																							
9.46	-1024	**LONGTOWN JCN**			10/56	11.06		11/31			11/51		12.36			13.42		13/51				14/51		16/19	15.54
14.03	+261	Riddings Jcn			11/05	11.20		11/40	12/00	12.06						13.51		14/00				15/00		16/31	16.02
16.49	+109	Penton						(To Lang-holm)					12.06 (To B. Bank)												16.08
21.11	-3299	Kershope Foot																							16.16
24.18	+605	Newcastleton							12.25	12.35						14.06							15.23	16.54	16.22
24.18		Newcastleton			11/27				12.30				12.52			14.07					14/22		15B29 (17.26)	16.23	
28.63	+85	Steele Road													13.42										16.33
32.27	+75	**RICCARTON JCN**													13.49										16.42
32.27		**RICCARTON JCN**			12.02						13.07				13.49	14/26					14/57		16/07		16.43
34.40	+91	Whitrope Summit			12.10						13.15				13/55	14/31					15/05		16/15		16.47
38.28	-81	Shankend														14.01									16.57
41.39	-98	Stobs														14.08									17.03
42.68	-79	Stobs Camp																			15.30	15.50			
45.28	-99	**HAWICK**			12.38						13.43				14.15	14.47						16.00	16.42		17.10
45.28		**HAWICK**			13.20						14.10					14.53					16.15		16.35 (18.05)		17.16
49.52	+260	Hassendean																			16.23				17.23
53.02	-1413	Belses																			16.30				17.29
56.23	-573	Charlesfield																			16.37				17.36
57.50	-348	**ST BOSWELLS JCN**														15.09									17.36
57.50		**ST BOSWELLS JCN**			13.47						14.38					15.13							17.02		17.40
60.78	-1812	Melrose														15.20									17.47
64.52	+785	**GALASHIELS**														15.27									17.53
64.52		**GALASHIELS**			14.01						14.53					15.31					16.06		17.16		17.57
65.55	+115	Kilknowe Jcn																			16.08				
68.33	+116	Bowland																							18.06
71.43	+169	Stow																							18.15
75.50	+224	Fountainhall																							18.23
79.06	+122	Heriot		14.30																					18.30
80.19	+192	Falahill		14.35		14/46	14.50				15.38					15/54			16.05				18/01		18.33
82.14	-73	Tynehead					15.00		15.10 (Shunt																18.37
85.34	-70	Fushiebridge							15.30	15.40 for															
86.14	-70	Gorebridge								15.45 244)									16.05						18.44
88.38	-83	Newtongrange																							
89.74	-79	Hardengreen Jcn		15.00		15/13												16.26	16/33				18/26		18.51
90.19	-226	Eskbank																							18.53
91.76	-196	Millerhill Jcn																							
93.62	-259	Niddrie S. Jcn			15/12	15/21										16/12			16/41				18/34		18.58
95.15	-112	Portobello														16/14									19.02
98.15	+166	**EDINBURGH (WAV)**														16.20									19.08
		Destination			Niddrie	Niddrie										A'deen	E'bro						Niddrie		
		Due			15.18	15.26										17.49							18.39		

6

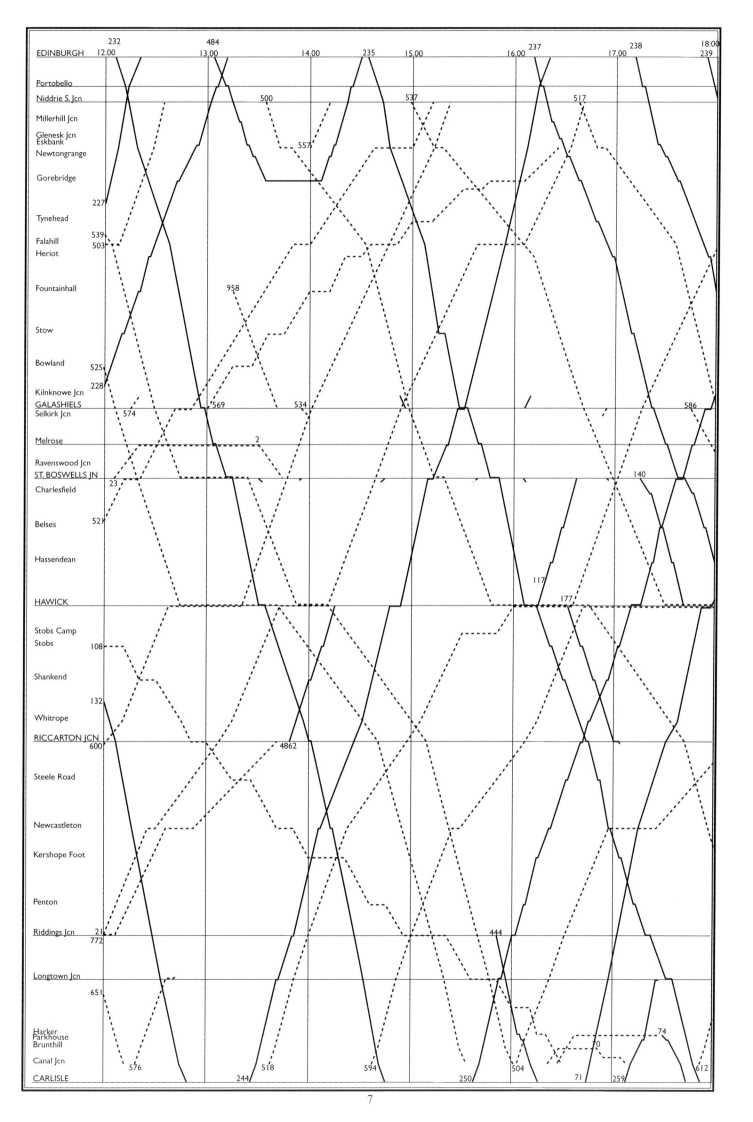

WORKING TIMETABLE (PASSENGER & GOODS) - EDINBURGH (WAV) to CARLISLE : 1953

Train / From (by column): 17.05 E'bro (238/354) · 16.35 Niddrie (517) · 18.10 S. Leith (547) · 15.55 D'dee W. (558) · 19.27 P'bello (16) · 22.28 Niddrie (502) · 22.20 Leith W. (562)

m.ch	Station	1/in	238	354	33	239	517	86	547	240	144	Light	558	575	557	558	16	243	558	502	502	5	562
	Class		B	B	LE	A	E	H	F	B	ECS	Light	E	C	C	E	A	A	E	EBV	H	LE	H
	Engine		V1	V1		D49	A3	K3	J36	B1	B1	B1	K3	V2	V2	K3	A3	A4	K3	J37	J37	J36	J36
0.00	EDINBURGH (WAV)			17.10		17.53				19.02				20.03	20.50		21.53	22.15					
3.00	Portobello	-166		17.16		17.59		18/34		19.11			19.27	20.10	20.57		21.59	22.21					23/07
4.33	Niddrie S. Jcn	+112		17.19				18/43		19.14			19.34	20.14	21.01		22.01	22.23		22/33			23/15
6.19	Millerhill Jcn	+259								19.18													
7.76	Eskbank	+196		17.25		18.01				19.23													
8.21	Hardengreen Jcn	+226							18.55				19.44	20.22									23.28
8.21	Hardengreen Jcn			17.26		18.06				19.24			19B50	20B35	21.07		22.06	22.29		22/40			
9.56	Newtongrange	+79		17.30																			
12.01	Gorebridge	+83		17.37						19.34													
12.61	Fushiebridge	+70																					
16.01	Tynehead	+70																					
17.76	Falahill	+73		17.52		18.26				19/48			20/33	21/11	21/41		22/25	22/49		23.05	23.15	23.30	
19.09	Heriot	-192		17.55						19.51													
22.45	Fountainhall	-122		18.01																			
26.52	Stow	-224		18.08		18.37																	
29.62	Bowland	-169																					
32.40	Kilknowe Jcn	-116			18/37																		
33.43	GALASHIELS	-115		18.19	18.39	18.47				20.09							22.43	23.08				23.55	
33.43	GALASHIELS					18.49				20.13			20.59	21.31	22.02		22.47	23.13		23/50			
37.17	Melrose	-785				18.57				20.20							22.54	23.21					
40.45	ST BOSWELLS JCN	+1812				19.03				20.26			21.14					23.27		00.09			
40.45	ST BOSWELLS JCN					19.06		19.17		20.29			(22.25)	21/41	22/12	22.25	22/59	23.31		00.20			
41.72	Charlesfield	+348																					
45.13	Belses	+573								20.38													
48.43	Hassendean	+1413								20.45													
52.67	HAWICK	-260				19.21		19.51		20.52				22.01	22.32	22.54	23.14	23.46		00.54			
52.67	HAWICK					19.26	19B35	20.00		21.20				22B20	22.45	(00.15)	23.19	00.00	00B15				
55.27	Stobs Camp	+99																					
56.56	Stobs	+79								21.29													
59.67	Shankend	+98								21.38													
63.55	Whitrope Summit	+81				19/51	20/30	21/05		21/45					22/55	23/20	23/43	00/26	01/05				
65.68	RICCARTON JCN	-91						21.08		21.48													
65.68	RICCARTON JCN					19.45	19/54	20/33		21.24	21.55				22/58	23.23	23.46	00.29	01.08				
69.32	Steele Road	-75																					
73.77	Newcastleton	-85					20.05				22.07												
73.77	Newcastleton					19/57	20.06	20.47		21/46		22.30			23/08	23/33	23/56	00/39	01/22				
77.04	Kershope Foot	-605																					
81.46	Penton	+3299																					
84.12	Riddings Jcn	-109						21/03	22/10														
88.49	LONGTOWN JCN	-261					20/15	20/26	21/12	22/19		22/50			23/27	23/52	00/13	00/56	01/47				
90.52	Fauldmoor	-556																					
91.46	Lyneside	+558																					
93.64	Harker	+316																					
94.18	Parkhouse	-3153																					
95.05	Brunthill	-552						21/22	22/33			23/00			23/35	00.00		01/57					
96.68	Canal Jcn	-685					20/30	20/36	21/26	22/37		23/03			23/38	00/03	00/22	01/06	02/01				
97.18	Canal Yard						20.32		21.29	22.40		23.05			23.41	00.06			02.04				
98.15	CARLISLE	+455					20.40										00.26	01.10					
	Destination																	St. P					
	Due																	09.12					

WORKING TIMETABLE (PASSENGER & GOODS) - CARLISLE to EDINBURGH (WAV) : 1953

Train / From (by column): 08.50 St. P (71) · 14.35 Canal (594) · 16.00 Canal (506) · 16.30 N'ctle (4896) · 17.50 Canal (612) · 20.55 St. B (271) · 17.50 Canal (617) · 20.55 St. B (529)

m.ch	Station	1/in	31	74	71	259	594	586	275	506	504	4896	5	612	33	612	775	271	775	612	775	617	529	3
	Class		H	Light	A	B	E	K	B	E	H	B	H	E	B	E	B	E	J	A	J	E	E	F
	Engine		J39	J39	A3	LM4	K3	J36	V1	B1	K3	D30	J36	K3	D49	K3	J35	A3	J35	K3	J35	K3	K3	J35
0.00	CARLISLE				16.45	17.08									18.13			19.33						
(0.77)	Canal Yard		16.20	16.25												17.50						20.45	22.00	23.10
1.27	Canal Jcn	-455	16/23	16/29	16/49	17/12									18/17	17/52		19/37				20/47	22/02	23/13
3.10	Brunthill	+685	16.28													17/55						20/50	22/05	23/16
3.77	Parkhouse	+552													18.24									
4.31	Harker	+3153		16.36																				
9.46	LONGTOWN JCN	-1024			16/58	17.28						18.06			18.34			19.49				21/01	22/16	23/28
14.03	Riddings Jcn	+261				17.36						18.15			18.44			19.55				21/10	22/25	23/38
16.49	Penton	+109				(to																		
21.11	Kershope Foot	-3299				Lang-									18.57									
24.18	Newcastleton	+605				holm)									19.02			20.09				21.35	22.50	
24.18	Newcastleton				17/15						17B26				19.03	19.16		20.10				21B39	22B54	00/03
28.63	Steele Road	+85																						
32.27	RICCARTON JCN	+75													19.22			20.27						
32.27	RICCARTON JCN				17/31					18/12	19.03					19/54		20.28				22/17	23/32	00/48
34.40	Whitrope Summit	+91			17/36					18/22	19/10						20/02	20/33				22/25	23/40	00/58
38.28	Shankend	-81									19.14													
41.39	Stobs	-98									19.20													
42.68	Stobs Camp	-79																						
45.28	HAWICK	-99			17.52					18.56	19.27					20.29		20.49				22.52	00.07	01.30
45.28	HAWICK				17.58			18.05		18.40	19.15					(21.29)		20.55			21.29	23.15	01.20	01.55
49.52	Hassendean	+260																						
53.02	Belses	-1413																						
56.23	Charlesfield	-573																						
57.50	ST BOSWELLS JCN	-348			18.14						19.09							21.11					01.49	02.28
57.50	ST BOSWELLS JCN				18.17		18/32	18.48		19.20	19/51						20.55	21.15			21.56		23.42	02.20
60.78	Melrose	-1812			18.24													21.22						
64.52	GALASHIELS	+785			18.30			19.09									21.15	21.28						
64.52	GALASHIELS				18.33		18/46		19.10	19/37		20.07		20.35				21.33	21.40	22/10			23/56	02/37
65.55	Kilknowe Jcn	+115							19/12															
68.33	Bowland	+116																						
71.43	Stow	+169																						
75.50	Fountainhall	+224																						
79.06	Heriot	+122																						
80.19	Falahill	+192			18/56		19/31			20/22	21/02		21.35					21/57	22/38	22/55			00/41	03/22
82.14	Tynehead	-73																						
85.34	Fushiebridge	-70																						
86.14	Gorebridge	-70																						
88.38	Newtongrange	-83																						
89.74	Hardengreen Jcn	-79			19.09		19/56			20/47	21/34							22/12	23.12	23/20	23.28		01/06	03/47
90.19	Eskbank	-226																						
91.76	Millerhill Jcn	-196																						
93.62	Niddrie S. Jcn	-259			19/14		20.07			20/55	21/44							22/17	23.28	23.42	01/14		03/55	
95.15	Portobello	-112			19/16						21.03							22/19						03.54
98.15	EDINBURGH (WAV)	+166			19.22													22.25						
	Destination						Meadows	E'bro			Niddrie							A'deen				Niddrie	Niddrie	
	Due						20.25	20.37			21.50							09.00				23.48	01.19	

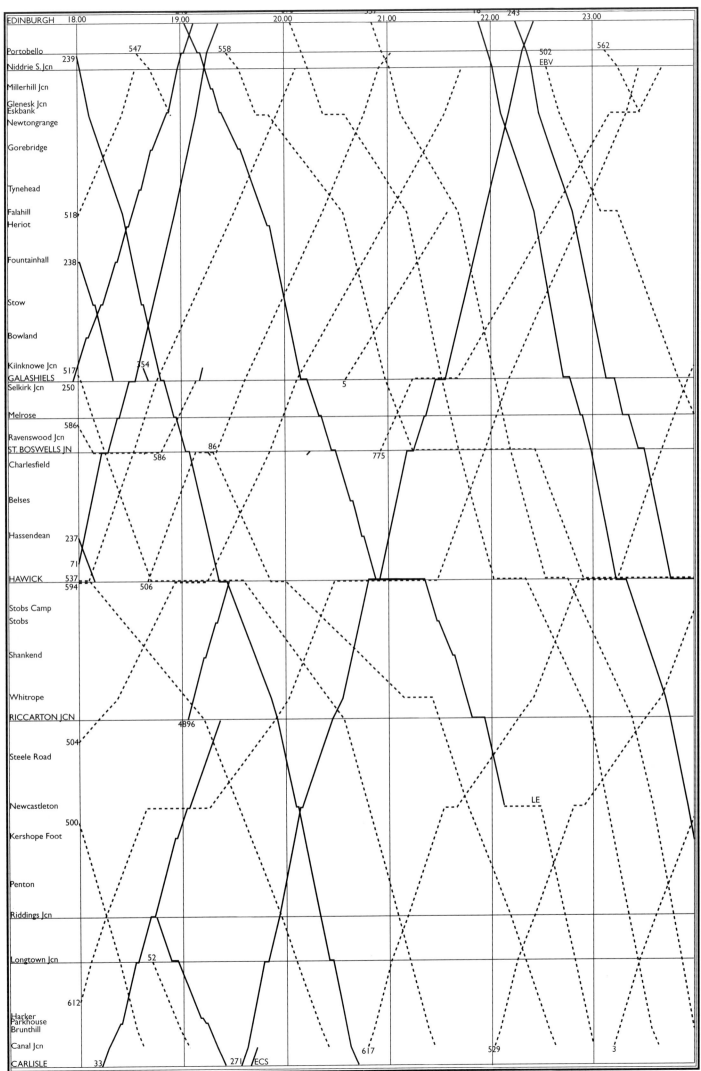

EDINBURGH 18.00 19.00 20.00 21.00 22.00 243 23.00
Portobello 547 558 502 562
239 EBV
Niddrie S. Jcn
Millerhill Jcn
Glenesk Jcn
Eskbank
Newtongrange
Gorebridge
Tynehead
Falahill 518
Heriot
Fountainhall 238
Stow
Bowland
Kilknowe Jcn 517 754
GALASHIELS
Selkirk Jcn 250 5
Melrose
586
Ravenswood Jcn
ST. BOSWELLS JN 86
586 775
Charlesfield
Belses
Hassendean 237
71
HAWICK 537
594 506
Stobs Camp
Stobs
Shankend
Whitrope
RICCARTON JCN 4896
504
Steele Road
Newcastleton LE
500
Kershope Foot
Penton
Riddings Jcn
Longtown Jcn 52
612
Harker
Parkhouse
Brunthill
Canal Jcn 617 529 3
CARLISLE 33 271 ECS

9

D34 62471 'Glen Falloch' of St Margaret's was no stranger to the Waverley route and spent much of the 1950's covering St Margarets diagrams based at Galashiels and at Hawick working from Riccarton Junction.   It is seen getting ready to leave Edinburgh Waverley for the south.

K3 2-6-0 61987 approaches Edinburgh with a down East Coast train seen using the Lothian Railways connection between Monktonhall Junction and Niddrie North Junction with a train for North Leith. The K3's were the standard goods engine on Waverley Route goods services with six of the class being used from St Margarets and four from Carlisle Canal.   They did not, however, have a total monopoly of Edinburgh - Carlisle goods workings and some services were handled by V2 2-6-2's, A3 Pacifics and B1 4-6-0's. (W.S.Sellar)

An important if little-known feature of Edinburgh was the Lothian Railway (Lothian Lines) which comprised a system of goods lines that allowed services to come from the direction of Edinburgh Waverley and connect with the Newcastle, Carlisle and Suburban lines without interfering with the main lines. One of the big (5F) J37 0-6-0's - 64538 of St Margarets - passes Niddrie North Junction in October 1955 and takes the Lothian Lines connection towards the east coast main line with a trip working from Portobello or Meadows. The train is probably taking empties to the Smeaton branch. (W.S.Sellar)

Haymarket's A2 Pacifics were not normally seen on the Waverley route but when shortages of A3's occurred they were as likely to be substituted as any other class. 60519 'Honeyway' passes under the Lothian Lines at Niddrie North Junction with the 14.33 Edinburgh - Carlisle semi-fast on the 17th October 1955. Normally the service was worked by a Haymarket A3 but the additional power of an A2 will not go amiss, especially as the return working is a class E goods trains from Carlisle Canal to Niddrie. In the background an N15 0-6-2T can just be seen to the left of the North Junction box. This has just finished banking an eastbound Lothian Lines train, the rear of which is to the right of 60519. (W.S.Sellar)

The passenger map of the Southern Uplands as it was in 1952, clearly showing - amongst much other detail - the relationship between the three routes between Edinburgh and England. The busiest of the trio was the East Coast route which on a normal 1953 weekday saw fifty-two southbound Anglo-Scottish services: fifteen passenger and thirty-seven goods. The level of service over the Waverley route was less than half this level (twenty-one southbound workings made up of fourteen goods and seven passenger services) although it carried considerably more traffic than the ex-Caledonian line via Beattock and Carstairs which had no more than two goods and five passenger Anglo-Scottish from Edinburgh to Carlisle and beyond.

With an advantage of three miles, the Caledonian route was much the faster of the two Edinburgh - Carlisle lines and where the morning Edinburgh to St Pancras express took two hours and forty-three minutes to reach Carlisle (and probably dropped five or ten minutes coughing its way to Falahill and Whitrope), the through expresses from Princes Street ran the distance in thirty to forty minutes less in spite of having to combine with a Glasgow portion at Symington or, latterly, Carstairs Junction.

The real strength of the Waverley route lay in goods traffic and while the Caledonian route was fully occupied in traffic going to and from Glasgow and Perth, almost all goods outside these two areas was routed via the North British main line, Niddrie and the Waverley route. It will be noticed from the Working Timetable that of the departures from Carlisle Canal Yard, one ran to Dundee while two each ran to Perth and Aberdeen.

The several branches that flowed from the main line owed more to optimism in the railway age although most of them managed to survive into the 1960's. The Riccarton Junction to Hexham line allowed the North British to boast that it was able to reach Newcastle independently of the East Coast route whilst the Tweedmouth - St Boswells branch was useful for Galashiels and Hawick traffic that had come down the East Coast. A third connection with the East Coast, from St Boswells to Reston, ceased to operate as a through line when a bridge was washed away during the storms of 1948. The stub between Reston and Duns survived for three years longer, a quiet memorial to the pre-1914 days when the first train of the day from St Boswells to Reston conveyed only passengers who had arrived from England by the through night express from St Pancras.

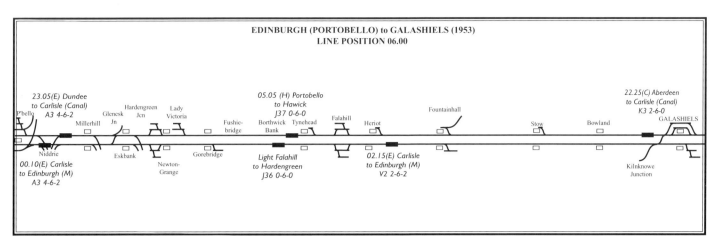

EDINBURGH (PORTOBELLO) to GALASHIELS (1953)
LINE POSITION 06.00

CONTROLLER'S LOG : Although well known for its scenic qualities, few enthusiasts - including those who have ridden on it - give the Waverley route much credit for conveying the traffic that it does. Since the public timetable scarcely covers two sides of paper this is hardly to be wondered at and compounding the issue is the fact that since the war the number of through trains to London has contracted to the morning and overnight expresses, a reduction

services from Carlisle to Edinburgh plus an interesting sprinkling of local services.

Operating goods trains is not the straightforward practice that it can be on other routes since the gradients between Edinburgh and Carlisle make the line one of the most exacting in the Kingdom to work; up trains having to be banked in rear from Hardengreen to Falahill, ten miles, and from Hawick to Whitrope; eleven miles while in the

where it will exchange crews with the 04.20 Carlisle to Portobello which is currently sitting at Riccarton Junction to allow the overnight sleeper from St Pancras to pass.

The standard express engine on the route is the A3 Pacific - examples from Carlisle and Haymarket share the principal diagrams - but the service currently between Melrose and Galashiels is the little-known daily instance of an A4 appearing on the line: one of the

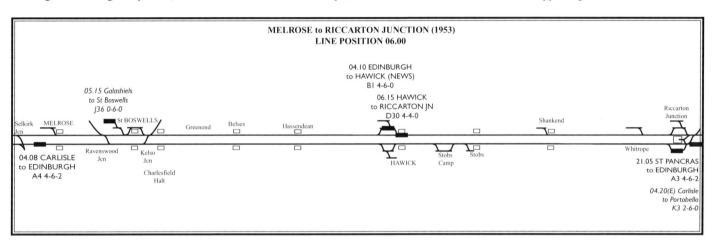

MELROSE to RICCARTON JUNCTION (1953)
LINE POSITION 06.00

that has done nothing to enhance the potential of the line. As a curious aside to this supposed economy, the former through trains continue to run as previously but terminate at Carlisle instead of continuing forward to Leeds and St Pancras. One wonders how much in the way of savings are realised, at least on the North British section, since during the 1930's the midday London train was handled by nothing grander than a D49 4-4-0 whilst today the Carlisle equivalent is provided with a full blown Pacific.

Passenger traffic may be a little thin on the ground at certain times of day but goods traffic makes good the shortfall with fourteen through

northbound direction trains have to be assisted over the eight mile section from Newcastleton to Riccarton Junction.

Naturally it goes without saying that one has to ensure that banking engines are in position in good time to assist main line services - two trains approaching Newcastleton in quick succession is an invitation to block the line for an hour or more - whilst another headache is provided by the fact that many of the through goods trains swap crews at Hawick or St Boswells.

This is the case with the 22.25 Aberdeen - Carlisle which is approaching Galashiels and should reach Hawick in about half an hour

Haymarket streamliners working the 22.15 Edinburgh - Carlisle and the 04.08 return. The A4 in question works quite a high daily mileage since its trip over the Waverley is made after working the 09.30 Glasgow (Queen St) - Kings Cross and the 10.10 Kings Cross - Glasgow between Edinburgh and Newcastle. The sight of such a celebrated visitor contrasts curiously with the everyday D30 4-4-0's that work most of the Hawick local passenger services. New B1 4-6-0's, such as the example that has arrived in Hawick with the Edinburgh News, make a few daily appearances but so far have kept away from the Waverley route sheds which continue to exude a pregrouping air.

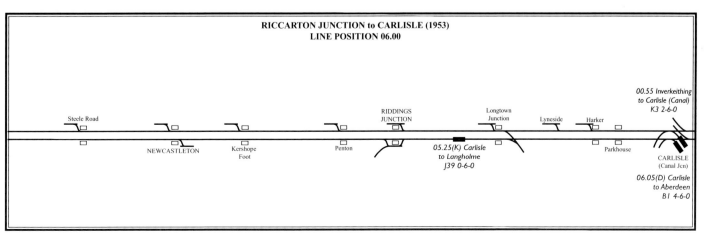

RICCARTON JUNCTION to CARLISLE (1953)
LINE POSITION 06.00

GALASHIELS

A small market town with a population of thirteen thousand, Galashiels was the first stop for the southbound expresses over the Waverley route as well as being the junction for the Selkirk and Peebles branches. The former, a six-mile connection with the county town, lost its passenger service in September 1951 which was rather a surprise since the prewar LNER had managed to maintain a service of eight return trips a day, latterly using Sentinel Railcar No.35 'Nettle'. Goods traffic survived however and provided employment for a J36 0-6-0 which did two trips per day over the branch.

The Peebles line branch was an alternative route to Edinburgh; promoted largely because the main line avoided the town of Peebles. By the early 1950's passenger services stood at four trains to Edinburgh via Peebles and three in the opposite direction. The imbalance arose because one of the workings, the 17.10 ex Edinburgh, ran via the main line. Goods traffic at the southern end of the Peebles line consisted of one working which arrived from Peebles at 11.40 and went back thirty-five minutes later after having its engine changed. (The Working Timetable for the line is on page 24).

Galashiels was also responsible for the working of the Lauder branch which had the distinction of being one of the few lines in the country over which any engine with a route availability of 2 or higher was prohibited. This brought to the main line the rather novel sight of tender-fitted Great Eastern J67 0-6-0T's as they ran the daily trip the eleven miles to Fountainhall where the branch - technically a light railway - commenced.

Galashiels shed was an outpost of Edinburgh St Margarets and had five daily bookings; the engines being changed by the parent shed when required. Two J36 0-6-0's were retained for the Selkirk and Peebles goods workings, a C15 4-4-2T worked the station pilot from 05.00 until 22.45 while a J67 was used for the Lauder light railway. In addition a V1 or V3 2-6-2T stabled overnight to work the first morning train to Edinburgh via Peebles.

Train	Engine	Dep	Destination	Train	Arr	Engine	Dep	Destination
22.05 Dundee West	A3 4-6-2	01/57	Carlisle (Canal)	11.35 Hawick	12.41	J37 0-6-0	12.50	Edinburgh (NIddrie)
22.00 Carlisle (Canal)	K3 2-6-0	02/37	Portobello	**12.05 EDINBURGH**	12.55	A3 4-6-2	12.57	**CARLISLE**
20.20 Aberdeen	K3 2-6-0	02/58	Carlisle (Canal)			J36 0-6-0	13.00	Hardengreen Junction
01.10 Carlisle (Canal)	A3 4-6-2	03/16	Dundee	12.15 Lauder	13.40	J67 0-6-0T		
01.00 Edinburgh (NIddrie)	J36 0-6-0		(Fwd at 03.40)			J36 0-6-0	13.55	Selkirk
00.55 Inverkeithing	K3 2-6-0	03/32	Carlisle (Canal)	10.40 Carlisle (Canal)		K3 2-6-0	14/01	Edinburgh (NIddrie)
01.30 Carlisle (Canal)	V2 2-6-2	03/36	Perth	11.35 Carlisle (Canal)		K3 2-6-0	14/53	Aberdeen
(01.00 Edinburgh (NIddrie))	J36 0-6-0	03.40	St Boswells	**13.18 EDINBURGH via Peebles**	14.54	V1 2-6-2T		
02.25 Portobello	D49 4-4-0	04.30	Hawick	13.30 Edinburgh (NIddrie)		K3 2-6-0	14/58	Carlisle (Canal)
00.10 Carlisle (Canal)	A3 4-6-2	04/31	Edinburgh (NIddrie)	**13.26 CARLISLE**	15.27	A3 4-6-2	15.31	**EDINBURGH**
04.10 EDINBURGH	B1 4-6-0	05.11	**HAWICK**	**14.33 EDINBURGH**	15.28	A3 4-6-2	15.32	**CARLISLE**
04.50 St Boswells	J36 0-6-0					V1 2-6-2T	16.06	**EDINBURGH via Peebles**
	J36 0-6-0	05.15	St Boswells EBV	14.55 Edinburgh (NIddrie)		K3 2-6-0	16/42	Carlisle (Canal)
02.15 Carlisle (Canal)	V2 2-6-2	05/23	Edinburgh (Meadows)	16.25 Selkirk	16.55	J36 0-6-0		
22.25 Aberdeen	K3 2-6-0	06/04	Carlisle (Canal)	13.35 Carlisle (Canal)		K3 2-6-0	17/16	Edinburgh (NIddrie)
04.08 CARLISLE	A4 4-6-2	06.09	**EDINBURGH**	**16.10 EDINBURGH**	17.21	B1 4-6-0	17.24	**HAWICK**
	J36 0-6-0	06.40	Selkirk			J36 0-6-0	17.45	St Boswells
05.05 Portobello	J37 0-6-0	06/49	Hawick	**15.37 CARLISLE**	17.53	B1 4-6-0	17.57	**EDINBURGH**
21.05 ST PANCRAS	A3 4-6-2	07.05	**EDINBURGH**	16.35 Edinburgh (NIddrie)		K3 2-6-0	18/02	Carlisle (Canal)
	V1 2-6-2T	07.13	**EDINBURGH via Peebles**	**17.10 EDINBURGH**	18.19	V1 2-6-2T		
06.44 HAWICK	D49 4-4-0	07.23	**EDINBURGH**	**08.50 ST PANCRAS**	18.30	A3 4-6-2	18.33	**EDINBURGH**
23.05 Dundee	A3 4-6-2	07/24	Carlisle (Canal)	**17.05 EDINBURGH via Peebles**	18.39	V1 2-6-2T		
06.35 EDINBURGH	B1 4-6-0	07.54	**CARLISLE**	14.35 Carlisle (Canal)		K3 2-6-0	18/46	Edinburgh (Meadows)
04.20 Carlisle (Canal)	K3 2-6-0	08/06	Portobello	**17.53 EDINBURGH**	18.47	A3 4-6-2	18.49	**CARLISLE**
08.07 EDINBURGH	B1 4-6-0	08.44	**EDINBURGH**	18.48 St Boswells	19.09	J36 0-6-0		
00.30 Dundee West	K3 2-6-0	08/57	Carlisle (Canal)			V1 2-6-2T	19.10	**EDINBURGH via Peebles**
08.35 Selkirk	J36 0-6-0			18.40 Hawick		B1 4-6-0	19/37	Portobello
06.05 Carlisle (Canal)	B1 4-6-0	09/21	Aberdeen	16.00 Carlisle (Canal)		K3 2-6-0	20/07	Edinburgh (NIddrie)
	J67 0-6-0T	09.26	Lauder	**19.02 EDINBURGH**	20.09	B1 4-6-0	20.13	**HAWICK**
07.56 EDINBURGH via Peebles	V1 2-6-2T					J36 0-6-0	20.35	Falahill
08.35 EDINBURGH	B1 4-6-0	09.49	**HAWICK**	19.27 Portobello		K3 2-6-0	20/59	Carlisle (Canal)
09.00 Hawick	J37 0-6-0	09/57	Portobello	20.55 St Boswells	21.15	J36 0-6-0		
	V1 2-6-2T	10.16	**EDINBURGH via Peebles**	**19.33 CARLISLE**	21.28	A3 4-6-2	21.33	**EDINBURGH**
08.00 Carlisle (Canal)	K3 2-6-0	10/50	Perth	15.55 Dundee (West)		V2 2-6-2	21/31	Carlisle (Canal)
10.05 EDINBURGH	A3 4-6-2	11.00	**ST PANCRAS**	(20.55 St Boswells)		J36 0-6-0	21.40	Edinburgh (NIddrie)
09.05 CARLISLE	A3 4-6-2	11.31	**EDINBURGH**	20.50 Edinburgh (Waverley Goods)		V2 2-6-2	22/02	Carlisle (Canal)
09.20 Peebles	J36 0-6-0			17.50 Carlisle (Canal)		K3 2-6-0	22/10	Aberdeen
11.11 HAWICK	B1 4-6-0	11.55	**EDINBURGH**	**21.53 EDINBURGH**	22.43	A3 4-6-2	22.47	**ST PANCRAS**
10.30 Portobello	K3 2-6-0	12/05	Carlisle (Canal)	**22.15 EDINBURGH**	23.08	A4 4-6-2	23.13	**CARLISLE**
09.00 Hardengreen	J36 0-6-0			23.15 Falahill		J37 0-6-0	23/50	Hawick
	J36 0-6-0	12.15	Peebles	Light ex Falahill	23.55	J36 0-6-0		
01.00 Aberdeen	K3 2-6-0	12/29	Carlisle (Canal)	20.45 Carlisle (Canal)		K3 2-6-0	23/56	Edinburgh (NIddrie)

TRAIN AND TRAFFIC WORKING : GALASHIELS (1953)

The V1 and V3 2-6-2 tanks managed much of the North British suburban service but were not prominent on the Waverley route although a few could be seen at Galashiels where they worked the passenger service via Peebles. It is a matter of regret that none could be spared for the branches radiating from the Waverley route - they were powerful and reliable engines - and a trip to Edinburgh was necessary to see the class in any numbers. 67662 of Glasgow (Parkhead) brings a train of parcels stock into Edinburgh Waverley. This engine arrived with the 07.37 ex Hyndland and remained in Edinburgh until leaving with the 16.48 back to Hyndland.

By 1965 steam was very much on the retreat in North British territory. Express passenger traffic was almost entirely in the hands of diesels - the BR fleet was all but complete - while most of the class 2 services had been taken over by multiple units and it took quite a stroke of fortune to find a service that was worked by steam south of Dundee. Odd pockets of steam - St Margarets and Dalry Road - remained for goods workings in the Edinburgh district and so long as they survived (and so long as diesels continued to display their rather dubious availability), there was always a chance that a steam engine might be booked to a passenger diagram at the last minute. This was the case on 19th May 1965 when the 12.00 (Saturdays Only) Hawick to Edinburgh semi-fast was captured behind B1 61244 climbing the 1 in 122 bank on the approach to Heriot. It was too much to hope that the corresponding 13.00 (Sats) Waverley to Hawick would be similarly powered and, rather predictably, it turned up behind a 1160hp D53xx Type 2. The two through St Pancras - Edinburgh workings had by that time been taken over by Sulzer 2500hp Type 4 diesel-electrics. (W.S.Sellar)

15

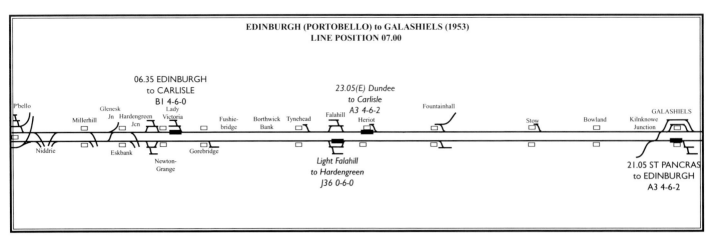

EDINBURGH (PORTOBELLO) to GALASHIELS (1953)
LINE POSITION 07.00

CONTROLLER'S LOG: The new B1 4-6-0's have only a handful of turns on the line and the 06.35 ex Edinburgh not only produces one of the Haymarket allocation but presents an interesting juxtaposition of forces since the class E goods train ahead of it is worked by a Pacific from the same shed. The reasoning behind this reversal of normal procedure gives credit to the higher power classification of the A3 but overlooks the lapses in adhesion that Pacifics can suffer from. The B1's, by contrast, are relatively stable machines.

booked to a D49 4-4-0. At one time these engines were a familiar sight but since the war they have tended to fade from view although they sometimes turn up on the Newcastle - Riccarton services when the supply of D30 4-4-0's dries up.

The 06.44 from Hawick continues to be diagrammed to a Haymarket member of the class; the engine working out with the 02.25 Portobello - Hawick goods. Careful attention has to be given to the 02.25 since the Edinburgh engine crew hand the D49 over to a set of local

- Carlisle and the 04.20 Carlisle - Edinburgh goods trains which are booked to meet at Hawick and exchange footplatemen. A similar watch has to be kept on the 23.05 Dundee - Carlisle (passing Heriot) and the 06.05 Carlisle - Aberdeen (Steele Road) which are also booked to exchange crews at Hawick.

Passenger traffic is much lighter at the Carlisle end of the line and the only early morning train provided is the long-standing stopping service from Riccarton Junction which - rather sportingly - provides a connection into

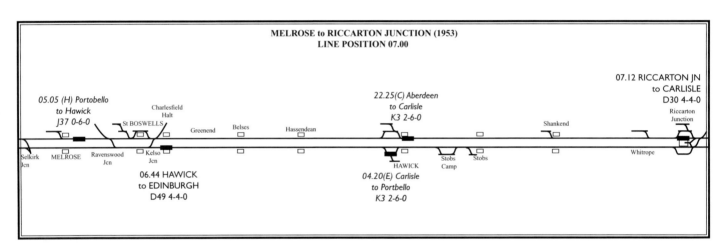

MELROSE to RICCARTON JUNCTION (1953)
LINE POSITION 07.00

Unless called upon to cover an emergency, the 4-6-0 will sit on Carlisle Canal shed until ringing off to work the 15.37 stopping train to Edinburgh. The A3, on the other hand, follows a much more adventurous diagram since it works the 14.00 express from Carlisle to Newcastle and the 17.20 slow train back. It then spends the night on Carlisle Canal loco before taking over the St Pancras overnight sleeper from a Holbeck 5XP 4-6-0.

Another interesting working is the first of the two business trains from Hawick to Edinburgh - now at Charlesfield - which is

men at Hawick and return to the Waverley with the Pacific of the 21.00 ex St Pancras.

The D49 is not seen again on the Waverley route after reaching Edinburgh and instead works a turn on the Corstorphine branch before finishing with the 15.46 school train from Edinburgh to Larbert and the 17.37 return.

At this time of day, Hawick can be a fairly busy location. The overnight from London - one of the big events of the day - pulls away for Edinburgh at 06.27 and is followed a quarter of an hour later by the D49 and its train. Attention is then directed to the overnight Dundee

the morning Carlisle - Euston express. The engine for the local - D30 4-4-0 62432 'Quentin Durward' is a regular in the diagram - is based at Riccarton Junction and returns with the 09.45 local goods from Carlisle Canal.

Pulling out of Canal Yard is a J39 0-6-0 with the morning trip service to Hawick which serves Longtown, Newcastleton, Riccarton Junction, Stobs and Stobs Camp. If all goes to plan the train will keep ahead of the 08.00 Carlisle to Perth class D goods as far as Riccarton Junction and then scrape into Hawick just ahead of the 09.05 Carlisle - Edinburgh passenger.

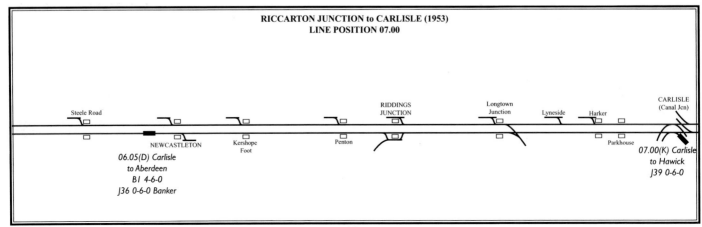

RICCARTON JUNCTION to CARLISLE (1953)
LINE POSITION 07.00

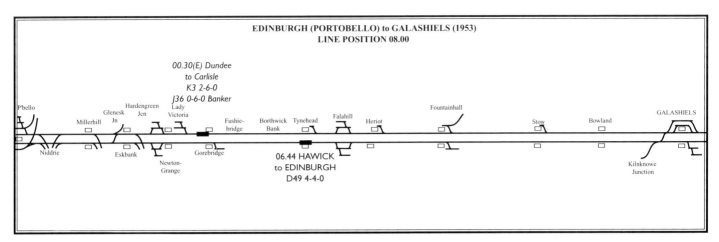

EDINBURGH (PORTOBELLO) to GALASHIELS (1953)
LINE POSITION 08.00

CONTROLLER'S LOG: As usual, Hawick is the focus of attention with the tension rising as it always does when two goods trains, booked to exchange footplates, approach. One of these services is cooling its heels at Stobs Camp as it waits for the 08.07 Hawick - Edinburgh passenger to get under way. Although appearing as a routine stopping train in the timetable, the 08.07 is one of the most - perhaps the most - important passenger trains on the route since it conveys the office

There are some interesting trains on the run between Riccarton Junction and Carlisle. The Riccarton D30 4-4-0 is nearing the end of its run to Carlisle while a Hawick-based member of the same class is pulling out of Newcastleton with a local for Hawick. This engine worked out by banking the 00.55 Inverkeithing - Carlisle class C goods to Whitrope and then ran light to Newcastleton where it picked up the stock of its train.

J39 'Standard' 0-6-0's are much more in

as a year or so ago. A J39 works the first part of the branch service which starts with the morning goods from Canal Yard, continues with a pair of passenger trips between Langholm and Riddings Junction and concludes with the 10.42 Langholm to Carlisle passenger. The afternoon turn is generally worked by 2-6-0 43139 which rings off Canal shed at 11.20 to run light to Langholm.

Another J39-worked branch is that from Longtown Junction to Gretna (Blackbank)

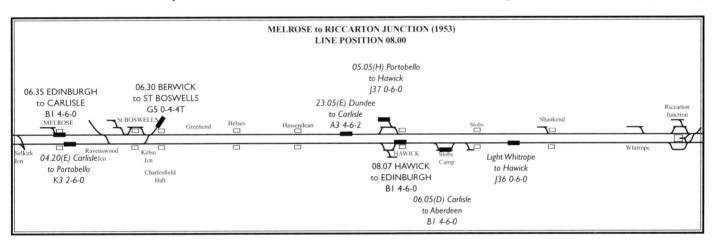

MELROSE to RICCARTON JUNCTION (1953)
LINE POSITION 08.00

aristocracy to work and its timekeeping can be a sensitive issue.

While noting that all the arrangements for the changeovers at Hawick are in place, one feels a pang of sympathy for the crew who have arrived with the 23.05 ex Dundee as they enquire about their return working - the 06.05 Carlisle to Aberdeen - and are given the engine number. A pause follows as they realise that the second part of their working is not going to be as easy as the first. The A3's are generally comfortable engines to work and reasonably easy to fire. The K3 is just the opposite and are notorious for their rough riding.

evidence at Carlisle than in the Edinburgh district and put in a fair amount of work of local work south of Riccarton Junction. One can be seen approaching Kershopefoot with the local Carlisle - Hawick goods while another heads the workman's train to Harker. This will be joined by a second train in half an hour which will combine and go forward empty at 08.30 to Riddings Junction to provide stock for the Langholm branch service; the engine then returning light to Carlisle to work the Longtown Junction/Gretna goods trip.

J39's are also associated with the seven-mile Langholm branch although not as much

whose sole service is a midday goods trip from Carlisle.

43139 owes its existence at Carlisle to the fact that the shed came under London Midland control for a brief time in 1950, during which period the shed's five class 4 engines - D49 4-4-0's - were disposed of.

Two D49's returned when the shed was restored to North British control but to increase the class 4 numbers, 43139 was sent new to Carlisle. As a result of there being almost no diagrammed work for class 4 engines, the 2-6-0 spent most of its days working opposite a class 5F J39 0-6-0 on the Langholm branch.

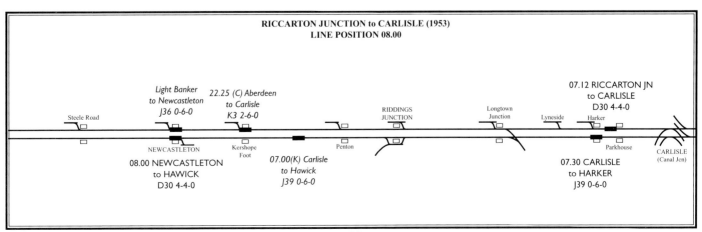

RICCARTON JUNCTION to CARLISLE (1953)
LINE POSITION 08.00

TRAFFIC WORKING : CARLISLE CANAL (1948)

Train	Canal	Class	Destination	Train	Canal	Class	Destination
	00.15		St Boswells	11.50 London Road	12.10	Canal 4 trip	(13.00)
	00.30	Canal 1 trip	Currock Jcn		12.15		**Blackbank**
	01.00	Canal 2 trip	Upperby	**11.28 Silloth**	12.49		
22.15 Newcastle (Addisons)	01.07				13.00	Canal 4 trip	London Road
	01.10		**Edinburgh (Niddrie)**	12.55 London Bridge	13.15	Canal 2 trip	(15.00)
Light ex Currock Yard	01.10	Canal 1 trip	(01.30)		13.45		**Edinburgh (Niddrie)**
01.05 Upperby	01.25	Upperby 9 trip	(02.00)		13.55		**Newcastle (Addisons)**
	01.30	Canal 1 trip	Durran Hill		14.15		**Silloth**
	02.00	Upperby 9 trip	Kingmoor	**10.35 Acomb Colliery**	14.16		
20.35 Edinburgh (Portobello)	02.01			13.05 Petteril Bridge	14.20	Upperby 15 trip	(15.15)
02.30 London Road	02.55	Canal 1 trip	(04.00)	**07.30 Edinburgh (Niddrie)**	14.28		
03.00 Petteril Bridge	03.20	Kingmoor 13 trip	(04.40)	14.15 Petteril Bridge	14.35	Kingmoor 13 trip	(14.40)
23.00 Edinburgh (Niddrie)	03.37				14.40	Kingmoor 13 trip	Light to shed
	04.00	Canal 1 trip	London Road	Light ex Kingmoor	14.52	Upperby 15 trip	(15.15)
04.00 Kingmoor	04.18	Kingmoor 2 trip	(05.00)		15.00	Canal 2 trip	Durran Hill
	04.35		**Edinburgh (Niddrie)**		15.15	Upperby 15 trip	Upperby
	04.40	Kingmoor 13 trip	Viaduct Yard	15.57 Kingmoor	16.12	Upperby 9 trip	(16.35)
04.30 Viaduct	04.45	Kingmoor 8 trip	(04.50)		16.20		**Brunthill**
	04.50	Kingmoor 8 trip	Light to shed	16.00 London Road	16.20	Canal 4 trip	(17.05)
02.00 Newcastle (Addisons)	04.52				16.35	Upperby 9 trip	London Road
	05.00	Kingmoor 2 trip	Upperby	**15.00 Silloth**	16.45		
00.50 Edinburgh (Niddrie)	05.34			**16.50 Brunthill**	17.00		
	05.35		Langholme		17.05	Canal 4 trip	London Road
05.30 Dentonholme	05.42	Kingmoor 12 trip	(06.00)	Light ex Viaduct	17.25	Kingmoor 14 trip	(18.10)
	06.00		**Silloth**	17.30 Petteril Bridge	17.48	Kingmoor 5 trip	(18.20)
	06.00	Kingmoor 12 trip	Durran Hill		18.10	Kingmoor 14 trip	Durran Hill
Light engine	06.45	Canal 5 trip	London Road	**11.40 Edinburgh (Niddrie)**	18.15		
	06.50	Canal 3 trip	London Road		18.20	Kingmoor 5 trip	Dentonholme
06.40 Viaduct	06.55	Canal 1 trip	(07.50)	18.10 Upperby	18.30	Upperby 11 trip	(19.10)
	07.10		**Edinburgh (Niddrie)**	18.25 Viaduct	18.40	Kingmoor 7 trip	(20.00)
	07.15		**Acomb Colliery**	**10.07 Liverpool (Aintree)**	18.50		
	07.50	Canal 1 trip	Upperby	**14.25 Blackbank**	18.55		
	08.00		**Hawick**		19.00		**Newcastle (Addisons)**
	08.42		**Silloth**		19.10		**Edinburgh (Meadows)**
09.00 London Bridge	09.20	Canal 1 trip	(09.50)		19.10	Upperby 11 trip	Upperby
04.39 Edinburgh (Niddrie)	09.23			18.50 Upperby	19.10	Kingmoor 2 trip	(19.15)
	09.50		**Riccarton Jcn**		19.15	Kingmoor 2 trip	Light to shed
	09.50	Canal 1 trip	Viaduct Yard	**13.25 Edinburgh (Niddrie)**	19.40		
	09.55		**Brunthill**	Light ex London Road	19.40	Canal 4 trip	To Shed
	10.15		**Edinburgh (Portobello)**		20.00	Kingmoor 7 trip	London Road
10.05 Upperby	10.20	Upperby 3 trip	(10.50)	**20.00 Silloth**	21.05		
	10.50	Upperby 3 trip	Durran Hill	20.45 London Road	21.05	Canal 3 trip	To Shed
10.40 Viaduct	10.53	Canal 1 trip	(11.30)		21.25		**Edinburgh (Portobello)**
10.50 Brunthill	11.03			**18.35 Newcastle (Addisons)**	21.27		
	11.25		**Edinburgh (Meadows)**	Light ex Viaduct	21.42	Kingmoor 12 trip	(22.50)
Light ex Viaduct	11.25	Canal 2 trip	(12.00)		22.30		**Newcastle (Addisons)**
	11.30	Canal 1 trip	Upperby		22.50	Kingmoor 12 trip	Upperby
	11.35		**Silloth**		22.55		**Edinburgh (Niddrie)**
	12.00	Canal 2 trip	London Road	**19.40 St Boswells**	23.00		
02.50 Orsall Lane (Manchester)	12.06			**19.10 Edinburgh (Waverley)**	23.03		

Most enthusiasts think of Carlisle as being the Citadel passenger station even though it probably did not account for more than one per cent of local activity even on the busiest of days.

The arrangements for goods traffic were exactly the opposite to those of passenger and where the six companies using the area had a common passenger station, each had its own marshalling yard which meant that inward trains terminated on one side of Carlisle whilst starting services commenced, several miles away, on the other with the local administration having the task of both sifting and shifting the thousands of goods wagons that arrived in the area each day.

The magnitude and complexity of the task can be gauged from the map opposite. A Midland train terminating in Petteril Bridge Yard on the South Eastern corner of the City might contain ten wagons for the Caledonian, ten for the North British, ten for the Maryport and Carlisle, ten for the North Eastern, ten for the Glasgow & South Western and ten for Carlisle itself. Few of these would be grouped together in the train as it arrived in Carlisle and as soon as it came to a stand, the train would have to be broken up into sections for the various yards on the other side of the city.

Thus one train would form five or six others

with the process being continuously repeated at each of the other yards as trains arrived and were broken up into their component parts.

Having assembled a series of trains at Petteril Bridge (Midland) for Viaduct (Caledonian), Canal (North British), Currock Junction (Maryport & Carlisle), Dentonholme (G&SWR) and Upperby (LNWR) yards, engines, crews and guards were needed to move them - as speedily as possible - across the city and this task was such that no less than twenty engines were more or less continuously engaged in tripping traffic from one yard to another.

In typical LMS fashion, everything was planned to several places of decimals and instead of being marked 'as required' as might have been the case on the North Eastern, the transfer engines were timed with the same precision as the Euston suburban service; any extemporisation - which could be considerable - being left to the Yard Inspectors and the District Controller.

The timing office worked on the assumption that each yard would always have a trainload of traffic for every other yard whilst in reality Upperby, for example, might at any given time have three trains for Kingmoor but nothing for Canal while in the meantime it might be evident that if Petteril Bridge was not cleared of its Dentonholme traffic, a block would have to be

put on main line trains approaching Carlisle on the Midland - something that would have been unthinkable - and it was little wonder that the Carlisle Controller tended to live on his nerves.

At midday on a typical day he would have the following under his gaze (in addition, of course, to the main line traffic!). Target 1 should have arrived light at Upperby from Kingmoor to work a Caledonian train to Viaduct Yard whilst target 2 should be running into Kingmoor with a train from Petteril Bridge, its next load - a load of LNW's for Upperby - being ready in an adjacent road. Target 3 was en route from Durran Hill to Upperby, picking up LNW traffic at London Road on its way with Target 4 doing a stint of mainline work by running from Currock to Dalston on the Maryport & Carlisle. Target 5 was shunting in London Road yard and preparing the 14.05 exchange trip to Durran Hill; Target 6 working from Durran Hill to Kingmoor but attaching en route at Petteril Bridge.

Target 7 was shunting out coal empties at the power station prior to tripping them to Dentonholme whilst target 13 was getting ready to leave London Road with a train of Caledonians for Kingmoor. Target 14 was on its way to Viaduct Yard from Upperby and Target 15 shunted Petteril Bridge sidings and put together the 13.05 to Canal Yard. Targets

10,11 and 12 were still on shed.

On top of the twelve LMS trips there were three of the five North British target engines at work: Canal 2 pulling out of Canal Yard with a train for London Road, Canal 4 en route from London Road to Canal and Canal 5 leaving London Road for Currock Yard.

Simply keeping track of the trip movements was a fulltime job yet this was secondary to ensuring that they were kept in gainful employment; a task best accomplished by knowing in detail the traffic that was pouring into the yards and being able to stay a step or two ahead of events.

With all these trains operating in an area no more than three miles long, congestion on the running lines was an ever-present danger and the odds were stacked in favour of delay. Indeed it is doubtful if a trip from the extremities - Upperby to Canal - ever completed its run without suffering prolonged signalling delays whilst only in the most dire of circumstances could a train be routed via the Citadel which had almost nothing in the way of facilities for dealing with slow goods services. (In common with many of the larger passenger stations on the London Midland, little short of an act of parliament was needed to get a goods train to pass on the passenger lines). Permissive block was in operation on most of the goods lines and although this eased the position

Canal No.1 Pilot N15 0-6-2T				Canal No.3 Pilot N15 0-6-2T			
Arr	Yard	Depart	Train	Arr	Yard	Depart	Train
	Shed	00.20	Light		Shed	06.50	Light
	Canal Yard	00.30	Trip	07.11	London Road	07.30	Trip
00.45	Currock Jcn	00.55	Light	07.50	Electric Works	08.25	Trip
01.10	Canal Yard	01.30	Trip	08.47	London Road	09.40	Trip
01.48	Durran Hill	02.05	Light	10.03	Electric Works	11.30	Trip
02.10	London Road	02.30	Trip	11.38	London Road	15.30	Trip
02.55	Canal Yard	04.00	Trip	15.52	Kingmoor	16.36	Trip
04.20	London Road	04.45	Trip	17.02	Upperby	18.00	Trip
04.55	Upperby	05.30	Trip	18.20	Viaduct	19.00	Trip
05.50	Viaduct	06.40	Trip	19.05	Dentonholme	19.40	Trip
06.55	Canal Yard	07.50	Trip	19.57	Upperby	20.00	Light
08.12	Upperby	08.20	Light	20.05	London Road	20.45	Trip
08.30	London Road	09.00	Trip	21.05	Canal Yard	21.10	Trip
09.20	Canal Yard	09.50	Trip	21.15	Shed		
10.05	Viaduct	10.40	Trip				
10.53	Canal Yard	11.30	Trip				
11.55	Upperby	12.20	Light				
12.30	Petteril Bridge						
	As required						

				Canal No.4 Pilot N15 0-6-2T			
				Arr	Yard	Depart	Train
Canal No.2 Pilot N15 0-6-2T					Shed	11.20	Light
Arr	Yard	Depart	Train		London Road	11.50	Trip
	Shed	00.40	Light	12.10	Canal Yard	13.00	Trip
	Canal Yard	01.00	Trip	13.25	London Road	16.00	Trip
01.20	Upperby	02.00	Trip	16.20	Canal Yard	17.05	Trip
02.20	Viaduct	02.35	Light	17.27	London Road	19.15	Trip
02.44	Kingmoor	03.15	Trip	19.40	Canal Yard	19.45	Light
03.39	Durran Hill	03.45	Trip	19.50	Shed		
03.50	Petteril Bridge	04.10	Trip				
04.35	Kingmoor	05.00	Trip				
05.23	Durran Hill	05.45	Trip	Canal No.5 Pilot N15 0-6-2T			
05.50	London Road	06.20	Trip	Arr	Yard	Depart	Train
06.45	Viaduct	06.50	Light		Shed	06.35	Light
06.55	Dentonholme	07.05	Trip		Canal Yard	06.45	
07.25	Upperby	07.40	Trip	07.05	London Road	09.20	Trip
08.00	Viaduct	08.15	Light	09.35	Currock Jcn	10.40	Trip
08.20	Dentonholme	08.45	Trip	11.00	London Road	12.00	Trip
09.00	Currock Jcn	09.45	Trip	12.20	Currock Jcn	13.00	Trip
10.05	Upperby	10.45	Trip	13.20	London Road	17.40	Trip
11.05	Viaduct	11.15	Light	17.55	Currock Jcn	19.25	Trip
11.25	Canal Yard	12.00	Trip	19.40	London Road	20.25	Trip
12.17	London Road	12.55	Trip	20.40	Currock Jcn	21.30	Trip
13.15	Canal Yard	15.00	Trip	21.48	London Road	21.55	Light
15.22	Durran Hill	15.30	Light	22.10	Shed		
15.50	Shed						

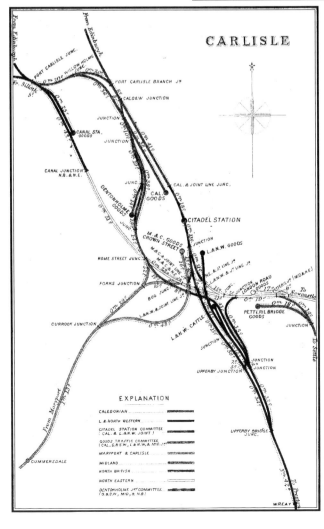

a little, the chances of the running times being met were slim.

Traffic coming into the North British Canal Yard at Carlisle could be destined for any destination west of the Pennines and apart from loads of exceptional importance for which details were given to the yard by the Controller, the first the Yard inspector knew of a wagon's destination was when he looked at the wagon label.

Generally, traffic flows followed a pre-grouping pattern with thirteen of the twenty-five trips from Canal running to London Road or Durran Hill with traffic for the North Eastern and Midland respectively. Seven trips ran to Upperby, conveying traffic from North British stations to LNWR destinations and the Great Western via Crewe. (The London Midland ran several through services from Upperby to Gresty Lane, Crewe).

The remaining five trips conveyed 'odds and sods' traffic to Currock Junction, Kingmoor, Viaduct and Dentonholme.

The trip working was generally handled by N15 0-6-2T's, Caledonian 0-6-0T's and LMS 3F 0-6-0T's for Canal, Kingmoor and Upperby respectively.

Much of the North British trip working was operated by N15 0-6-2 tanks at both ends of the line. 69222 of St Margaret's comes off one train at Niddrie and waits instructions for the next. (W.S.Sellar)

Engine	Class	Aug-50	Sep-50	Oct-50	Nov-50	Dec-50	Jan-51	Feb-51	Mar-51	Apr-51	May-51	Jun-51	Jul-51
64539	5F: J37 0-6-0 (1914)												
62417	3P: D30 4-4-0 (1912)						W/D	X	X	X	X	X	X
62420	3P: D30 4-4-0 (1912)												
62422	3P: D30 4-4-0 (1912)												
62423	3P: D30 4-4-0 (1912)												
62425	3P: D30 4-4-0 (1912)												
62428	3P: D30 4-4-0 (1912)												
62432	3P: D30 4-4-0 (1912)												
62435	3P: D30 4-4-0 (1912)	X	X	X	X	X	Ex E'bro (SM)						
62440	3P: D30 4-4-0 (1912)												
64463	3F: J35 0-6-0 (1906)												
64494	3F: J35 0-6-0 (1906)												
64509	3F: J35 0-6-0 (1906)												
67457	2P: C15 4-4-2T (1911)												
67459	2P: C15 4-4-2T (1911)												
67465	2P: C15 4-4-2T (1911)												
67472	2P: C15 4-4-2T (1911)												
67477	2P: C15 4-4-2T (1911)												
65232	2F: J36 0-6-0 (1888)												
65242	2F: J36 0-6-0 (1888)												
65259	2F: J36 0-6-0 (1888)												
65279	2F: J36 0-6-0 (1888)								W/D	X	X	X	X
65316	2F: J36 0-6-0 (1888)	X	X	X	X	X	X	X	X	Ex E'bro (SM)			
65317	2F: J36 0-6-0 (1888)												
65340	2F: J36 0-6-0 (1888)												
68138	0F: Y1 0-4-0T (1925)												

Engine	Class	Aug-51	Sep-51	Oct-51	Nov-51	Dec-51	Jan-52	Feb-52	Mar-52	Apr-52	May-52	Jun-52	Jul-52
64539	5F: J37 0-6-0 (1914)												
62420	3P: D30 4-4-0 (1912)												
62422	3P: D30 4-4-0 (1912)												
62423	3P: D30 4-4-0 (1912)												
62425	3P: D30 4-4-0 (1912)												
62428	3P: D30 4-4-0 (1912)												
62432	3P: D30 4-4-0 (1912)												
62435	3P: D30 4-4-0 (1912)												
62440	3P: D30 4-4-0 (1912)												
64463	3F: J35 0-6-0 (1906)												
64494	3F: J35 0-6-0 (1906)												
64509	3F: J35 0-6-0 (1906)												
67457	2P: C15 4-4-2T (1911)												
67459	2P: C15 4-4-2T (1911)												
67465	2P: C15 4-4-2T (1911)												
67472	2P: C15 4-4-2T (1911)												
67477	2P: C15 4-4-2T (1911)												
65232	2F: J36 0-6-0 (1888)												
65242	2F: J36 0-6-0 (1888)												
65259	2F: J36 0-6-0 (1888)												
65316	2F: J36 0-6-0 (1888)												
65317	2F: J36 0-6-0 (1888)												
65331	2F: J36 0-6-0 (1888)	X	X	X	X	X	X	X	X	X	Ex Bathgate		
65340	2F: J36 0-6-0 (1888)						W/D	X	X	X	X	X	X
68138	0F: Y1 0-4-0T (1925)												

Engine	Class	Aug-52	Sep-52	Oct-52	Nov-52	Dec-52	Jan-53	Feb-53	Mar-53	Apr-53	May-53	Jun-53	Jul-53
64539	5F: J37 0-6-0 (1914)												
62420	3P: D30 4-4-0 (1912)												
62422	3P: D30 4-4-0 (1912)												
62423	3P: D30 4-4-0 (1912)												
62425	3P: D30 4-4-0 (1912)												
62428	3P: D30 4-4-0 (1912)												
62432	3P: D30 4-4-0 (1912)												
62435	3P: D30 4-4-0 (1912)												
62440	3P: D30 4-4-0 (1912)												
64463	3F: J35 0-6-0 (1906)												
64494	3F: J35 0-6-0 (1906)												
64509	3F: J35 0-6-0 (1906)												
67457	2P: C15 4-4-2T (1911)												
67459	2P: C15 4-4-2T (1911)												
67465	2P: C15 4-4-2T (1911)												
67472	2P: C15 4-4-2T (1911)												
67477	2P: C15 4-4-2T (1911)												
65232	2F: J36 0-6-0 (1888)												
65242	2F: J36 0-6-0 (1888)												
65259	2F: J36 0-6-0 (1888)												
65316	2F: J36 0-6-0 (1888)												
65317	2F: J36 0-6-0 (1888)												
65331	2F: J36 0-6-0 (1888)												
68138	0F: Y1 0-4-0T (1925)												

For at least halfway through the 1950's Hawick shed gave the impression of having resisted both the grouping and nationalisation; the only concession to change being an occasional change of number on a cabside and the use of a Sentinel (68138 of 1927) for the Kelso pilot. The allocation enjoyed an almost timeless status until 1955 up to which time the most major events consisting of D30 or J36 engines being imported from Edinburgh to replace those taken out of traffic.

The most serious sign of change came in 1954 when the shed's allocation of C15 4-4-2 tanks, which had not in postwar years enjoyed the best of mechanical health, were either withdrawn or transferred away. Expectations that a pair of 2-6-4 tanks which arrived from Polmadie and Perth in March 1955 were part of a replacement plan were misplaced since the two engines were intended for short-term duties on the Border Counties line which had been severed by floods near Hexham. The pair returned north after only a few weeks at Hawick. More permanent replacements for the five C15's came later in 1955 with the allocation of two C16 4-4-2T's whilst a pair of new BR Standard 2MT 2-6-0's, the latter probably being the first new engines to be sent to Hawick since the grouping, arrived to take over from the J36 Whitrope bankers: one operating between Hawick and Whitrope and the other between Newcastleton and Riccarton Junction.

In early 1956 one of the C16 4-4-2T's was withdrawn from traffic and was replaced by a V3 2-6-2T from St Margarets, the latter having been displaced by the decline in traffic over the Edinburgh suburban line. Another C15 replacement which arrived in early 1957 was an N2 0-6-2T which

Engine	Class	Aug-53	Sep-53	Oct-53	Nov-53	Dec-53	Jan-54	Feb-54	Mar-54	Apr-54	May-54	Jun-54	Jul-54
	LOCOMOTIVE ALLOCATION & MOVEMENTS : HAWICK (64G)												
64539	5F: J37 0-6-0 (1914)												
62420	3P: D30 4-4-0 (1912)												
62422	3P: D30 4-4-0 (1912)												
62423	3P: D30 4-4-0 (1912)												
62425	3P: D30 4-4-0 (1912)												
62428	3P: D30 4-4-0 (1912)												
62432	3P: D30 4-4-0 (1912)												
62435	3P: D30 4-4-0 (1912)												
62440	3P: D30 4-4-0 (1912)												
64463	3F: J35 0-6-0 (1906)												
64494	3F: J35 0-6-0 (1906)												
64509	3F: J35 0-6-0 (1906)												
67457	2P: C15 4-4-2T (1911)												
67459	2P: C15 4-4-2T (1911)						To Polmont	X	X	X	X	X	X
67465	2P: C15 4-4-2T (1911)												
67472	2P: C15 4-4-2T (1911)												
67477	2P: C15 4-4-2T (1911)												
65232	2F: J36 0-6-0 (1888)												
65242	2F: J36 0-6-0 (1888)						To E'bro (SM)	X	X	X	X	X	X
65259	2F: J36 0-6-0 (1888)												
65316	2F: J36 0-6-0 (1888)												
65317	2F: J36 0-6-0 (1888)												
65331	2F: J36 0-6-0 (1888)												
68138	0F: Y1 0-4-0T (1925)												

Engine	Class	8/54	9/54	10/54	11/54	12/54	1/55	2/55	3/55	4/55	5/55	6/55	7/55
	LOCOMOTIVE ALLOCATION & MOVEMENTS : HAWICK (64G)												
64539	5F: J37 0-6-0 (1914)												
80007	4MT 2-6-4T (1951)	X	X	X	X	X	X	X	Ex Polmadie	To Polmadie	X	X	X
42277	4MT 2-6-4T (1945)	X	X	X	X	X	X	X	Ex Perth	To Polmadie	X	X	X
62420	3P: D30 4-4-0 (1912)												
62422	3P: D30 4-4-0 (1912)												
62423	3P: D30 4-4-0 (1912)												
62425	3P: D30 4-4-0 (1912)												
62428	3P: D30 4-4-0 (1912)												
62432	3P: D30 4-4-0 (1912)												
62435	3P: D30 4-4-0 (1912)												
62440	3P: D30 4-4-0 (1912)												
64463	3F: J35 0-6-0 (1906)												
64494	3F: J35 0-6-0 (1906)												
64509	3F: J35 0-6-0 (1906)												
67495	2P: C16 4-4-2T (1915)	X	X	X	X	X	X	X	X	Ex E'bro (SM)			
67457	2P: C15 4-4-2T (1911)										W/D	X	X
67465	2P: C15 4-4-2T (1911)				W/D	X	X	X	X	X	X	X	X
67472	2P: C15 4-4-2T (1911)												
67477	2P: C15 4-4-2T (1911)		W/D	X	X	X	X	X	X	X	X	X	X
65232	2F: J36 0-6-0 (1888)												
65259	2F: J36 0-6-0 (1888)												
65316	2F: J36 0-6-0 (1888)												
65317	2F: J36 0-6-0 (1888)												
65331	2F: J36 0-6-0 (1888)												
68138	0F: Y1 0-4-0T (1925)												

Engine	Class	8/55	9/55	10/55	11/55	12/55	1/56	2/56	3/56	4/56	5/56	6/56	7/56
	LOCOMOTIVE ALLOCATION & MOVEMENTS : HAWICK (64G)												
64539	5F: J37 0-6-0 (1914)												
67606	4P: V3 2-6-2T (1930)	X	X	X	X	X	X	X	X	Ex E'bro (SM)			
67630	3P: V1 2-6-2T (1930)	X	X	X	X	X	X	Ex E'bro (SM)		To E'bro (SM)	X	X	X
62420	3P: D30 4-4-0 (1912)												
62422	3P: D30 4-4-0 (1912)												
62423	3P: D30 4-4-0 (1912)												
62425	3P: D30 4-4-0 (1912)												
62428	3P: D30 4-4-0 (1912)												
62432	3P: D30 4-4-0 (1912)												
62435	3P: D30 4-4-0 (1912)												
62440	3P: D30 4-4-0 (1912)												
64463	3F: J35 0-6-0 (1906)												
64494	3F: J35 0-6-0 (1906)												
64509	3F: J35 0-6-0 (1906)												
67489	2P: C16 4-4-2T (1915)	X	Ex Dundee										
67495	2P: C16 4-4-2T (1915)										W/D	X	X
67472	2P: C15 4-4-2T (1911)				To Polmont	X	X	X	X	X	X	X	X
78046	2MT 2-6-0 (1953)	X	X	NEW									
78047	2MT 2-6-0 (1953)	X	X	NEW									
65232	2F: J36 0-6-0 (1888)												
65259	2F: J36 0-6-0 (1888)				To Bathgate	X	X	X	X	X	X	X	X
65316	2F: J36 0-6-0 (1888)												
65317	2F: J36 0-6-0 (1888)												
65331	2F: J36 0-6-0 (1888)												
68138	0F: Y1 0-4-0T (1925)	To Ayr	X	X	X	X	X	X	X	X	X	X	X

spent much of its time as the pilot at St Boswells.

The standard tender engine for local passenger work in the area had for many years been the D30 4-4-0 of which eight were allocated to Hawick. Their declining mechanical condition and the closure of the Border Counties line combined to end their long spell in office and for a year from the Spring of 1958 some of their duties were handled by a pair of D34 Glen 4-4-0's, a class uncommon south of Edinburgh. The D34's, which were withdrawn in April 1959, proved to be the last North British 4-4-0's to operate from Hawick since the D30's were taken out of traffic at the end of 1958. After a few months in which the shed had no 4-4-0's on its books, D34 62488 'Glen Aladale' arrived from Edinburgh St Margarets in November 1959 and representatives of the class remained in situ for another two years. The last of the class to work from Hawick was 62484 'Glen Lyon' which remained in traffic until 1961.

A handful of LNER D49 4-4-0's were sent to the shed in 1959 but there was little work remaining for them and their appearance was little more than a last gasp by the 4-4-0 in the region. So long as steam operated the through goods workings between Edinburgh and Carlisle, banking assistance was necessary over Whitrope and the J36 0-6-0's remained operational at Hawick into the early 1960's until dieselisation made banking unnecessary.

LOCOMOTIVE ALLOCATION & MOVEMENTS : HAWICK (64G)

Engine	Class	Aug-56	Sep-56	Oct-56	Nov-56	Dec-56	Jan-57	Feb-57	Mar-57	Apr-57	May-57	Jun-57	Jul-57
64539	5F: J37 0-6-0 (1914)												
67606	4P: V3 2-6-2T (1930)												
69510	3P: N2 0-6-2T (1925)	X	X	X	X	X	X	Ex Parkhead					
62420	3P: D30 4-4-0 (1912)										W/D	X	X
62422	3P: D30 4-4-0 (1912)												
62423	3P: D30 4-4-0 (1912)												
62425	3P: D30 4-4-0 (1912)												
62428	3P: D30 4-4-0 (1912)												
62432	3P: D30 4-4-0 (1912)												
62435	3P: D30 4-4-0 (1912)												
62440	3P: D30 4-4-0 (1912)												
64463	3F: J35 0-6-0 (1906)												
64494	3F: J35 0-6-0 (1906)												
64509	3F: J35 0-6-0 (1906)												
67489	2P: C16 4-4-2T (1915)												
78046	2MT 2-6-0 (1953)												
78047	2MT 2-6-0 (1953)												
65232	2F: J36 0-6-0 (1888)					To Polmadie	X	X	X	X	X	X	
65316	2F: J36 0-6-0 (1888)												
65317	2F: J36 0-6-0 (1888)												
65331	2F: J36 0-6-0 (1888)												

LOCOMOTIVE ALLOCATION & MOVEMENTS : HAWICK (64G)

Engine	Class	Aug-57	Sep-57	Oct-57	Nov-57	Dec-57	Jan-58	Feb-58	Mar-58	Apr-58	May-58	Jun-58	Jul-58
64539	5F: J37 0-6-0 (1914)												
43141	4MT 2-6-0 (1947)	X	X	X	X	X	X	X	X	X	X	X	Ex Polmont
67606	4P: V3 2-6-2T (1930)												
69510	3P: N2 0-6-2T (1925)												
62483	3P: D34 4-4-0 (1913)	X	X	X	X	X	X	Ex E'bro (SM)					
62494	3P: D34 4-4-0 (1913)	X	X	X	X	X	X	Ex E'bro (SM)					
62422	3P: D30 4-4-0 (1912)												
62423	3P: D30 4-4-0 (1912)					W/D	X	X	X	X	X	X	X
62425	3P: D30 4-4-0 (1912)											W/D	X
62428	3P: D30 4-4-0 (1912)												
62432	3P: D30 4-4-0 (1912)												
62435	3P: D30 4-4-0 (1912)					W/D	X	X	X	X	X	X	X
62440	3P: D30 4-4-0 (1912)											W/D	X
64463	3F: J35 0-6-0 (1906)												
64494	3F: J35 0-6-0 (1906)												
64509	3F: J35 0-6-0 (1906)												
67489	2P: C16 4-4-2T (1915)												
78046	2MT 2-6-0 (1953)												
78047	2MT 2-6-0 (1953)												
65316	2F: J36 0-6-0 (1888)												
65317	2F: J36 0-6-0 (1888)												
65331	2F: J36 0-6-0 (1888)												

LOCOMOTIVE ALLOCATION & MOVEMENTS : HAWICK (64G)

Engine	Class	Aug-58	Sep-58	Oct-58	Nov-58	Dec-58	Jan-59	Feb-59	Mar-59	Apr-59	May-59	Jun-59	Jul-59
64539	5F: J37 0-6-0 (1914)												
43141	4MT 2-6-0 (1947)												
67606	4P: V3 2-6-2T (1930)											To E'bro (SM)	X
69510	3P: N2 0-6-2T (1925)												
62483	3P: D34 4-4-0 (1913)									W/D	X	X	X
62494	3P: D34 4-4-0 (1913)									W/D	X	X	X
62422	3P: D30 4-4-0 (1912)					W/D	X	X	X	X	X	X	X
62428	3P: D30 4-4-0 (1912)					W/D	X	X	X	X	X	X	X
62432	3P: D30 4-4-0 (1912)					W/D	X	X	X	X	X	X	X
64463	3F: J35 0-6-0 (1906)												
64494	3F: J35 0-6-0 (1906)												
64509	3F: J35 0-6-0 (1906)												
67489	2P: C16 4-4-2T (1915)												
78046	2MT 2-6-0 (1953)												
78047	2MT 2-6-0 (1953)												
78049	2MT 2-6-0 (1953)	X	X	X	X	X	X	X	X	X	X	Ex E'bro (SM)	
65233	2F: J36 0-6-0 (1888)	X	X	X	Ex Polmont								
65275	2F: J36 0-6-0 (1888)	Ex Polmont											
65316	2F: J36 0-6-0 (1888)	To Polmont	X	X	X	X	X	X	X	X	X	X	X
65317	2F: J36 0-6-0 (1888)												
65331	2F: J36 0-6-0 (1888)												

LOCOMOTIVE ALLOCATION & MOVEMENTS : HAWICK (64G)

Engine	Class	Aug-59	Sep-59	Oct-59	Nov-59	Dec-59	Jan-60	Feb-60	Mar-60	Apr-60	May-60	Jun-60	Jul-60
64539	5F: J37 0-6-0 (1914)				To E'bro (SM)	X	X	X	X	X	X	X	X
62712	4P: D49 4-4-0 (1927)	X	X	X	X			X	X	Ex T'ton Jcn			
62719	4P: D49 4-4-0 (1927)	X	X	X	Ex Haym't			W/D	X	X	X	X	X
62744	4P: D49 4-4-0 (1927)	X	X	X	X	X	X	X	X	Ex T'ton Jcn			
43141	4MT 2-6-0 (1947)												To Parkhead
69510	3P: N2 0-6-2T (1925)				W/D	X	X	X	X	X	X	X	X
62488	3P: D34 4-4-0 (1913)	X	X	X	Ex E'bro (SM)								
64463	3F: J35 0-6-0 (1906)				To E'bro (SM)	X	X	X	X	X	X	X	X
64494	3F: J35 0-6-0 (1906)												
64509	3F: J35 0-6-0 (1906)			W/D	X	X	X	X	X	X	X	X	X
67489	2P: C16 4-4-2T (1915)												
78046	2MT 2-6-0 (1953)												
78047	2MT 2-6-0 (1953)												
78049	2MT 2-6-0 (1953)												
65233	2F: J36 0-6-0 (1888)					To Bathgate	X	X	X	X	X	X	X
65275	2F: J36 0-6-0 (1888)												
65317	2F: J36 0-6-0 (1888)												
65331	2F: J36 0-6-0 (1888)												

MAIN LINE ENGINE WORKINGS

From LNER days until the arrival of diesels A3 Pacifics had been the invariable power for express services between Edinburgh and Carlisle but from 1960 with Type 4 diesels gradually taking over work on the East Coast, A1 and A2 Pacifics started to drift across to the Waverley route. A2 60534 'Irish Elegance' pulls away from Carlisle Canal Yard in July 1962 with the 11.32 class D (partially fitted) goods for Aberdeen (Craiginches) which it will work as far as Edinburgh. Until the arrival of diesel traction at Haymarket, 60534 had been engaged on workings between Edinburgh and Dundee. (W.S.Sellar)

Where passenger traffic was concerned, the Waverley route achieved a high degree of motive power standardisation with almost all Edinburgh - Carlisle services, fast and slow, being handled by A3 Pacifics. (This claim could also be extended to goods services which were almost invariably worked by the K3 2-6-0's).

With the summits of Falahill and Whitrope to be overcome the use of Pacifics commenced in early LNER days but did not extend beyond the through St Pancras services until after 1948 when the arrival of A1 and A2 Pacifics at Haymarket released a sufficiency of A3 locomotives to cover almost all services.

This generous use of Pacific power raised some eyebrows - not least amongst those who could remember 4-4-0's handling some of the prewar express services - but the conditions governing the line's operations were unusual. For one thing the weight of trains had increased considerably since 1939 - the area was well used by the armed forces for training - whilst there were greater restrictions on the amount of double-heading (an A3 or V2, for example, could only be assisted by a 4-4-0) than was the case on most lines.

Other types of Pacifics worked over the route from time to time but their appearances tended to be uncommon until the arrival of main line diesels at Haymarket from 1960 after which A1 and A2 engines became frequent visitors on both passenger and goods. One long-standing - and little known - exception to the rule of the A3's was that of a Haymarket A4 which nightly worked the 22.15 Edinburgh to Carlisle and the 04.08 return.

The workhorses of the line were the K3 2-6-0 'Jazzers' of which eight were based at Carlisle Canal and twenty-three at St Margarets. The importance - not to mention difficulties - of the Waverley being recognised by the fact that Carlisle Canal was the first North British shed to be given an allocation of the class when a batch of five engines arrived in 1924. (One of this early allocation - 61858 - was still operating from Canal in the early 1960's).

These powerful - class 6 - engines handled almost all the through goods services between Edinburgh and Carlisle with only a minority being worked by other - A3, V2 and B1 - classes while most local goods workings remained in the hands of NBR 0-6-0's.

Diagram	Class	Time	From	Destination	Arr	Comments
Haymarket 2	A4	10.10	Edinburgh	Newcastle	13.14	08.35 Glasgow - Kings Cross
Haymarket 2	A4	15.57	Newcastle	Edinburgh	18.26	10.05 Kings Cross - Glasgow
Haymarket 2	A4	22.15	Edinburgh	Carlisle	01.10	Passenger to Hawick.
Haymarket 2	A4	04.08	Carlisle	Edinburgh	07.02	Postal & Parcels
Haymarket 36A	A3	05.25	Haymarket Goods	Carlisle Canal	10.59	23.05 ex Dundee Class E Goods
Haymarket 36A	A3	14.00	Carlisle	Newcastle	15.43	
Haymarket 36A	A3	17.20	Newcastle	Carlisle	19.22	Stopping train
Haymarket 36B	A3	05.10	Carlisle	Edinburgh	07.54	21.05 ex St Pancras
Haymarket 36B	A3	14.33	Edinburgh	Carlisle	17.52	Stopping train
Haymarket 36B	A3	00.10	Carlisle Canal	Niddrie West	05.54	Class E goods
Haymarket 36C	A3	12.05	Edinburgh	Carlisle	14.45	
Haymarket 36C	A3	19.33	Carlisle	Edinburgh	22.25	Works 36A
Haymarket 37	B1	06.35	Edinburgh	Carlisle	10.29	Stopping train
Haymarket 37	B1	15.37	Carlisle	Edinburgh	19.08	Stopping train
Haymarket 38	V2	19.52	Haymarket Goods	Carlisle Canal	23.41	15.55 Dundee West - Carlisle Class C Goods
Haymarket 38	V2	02.15	Carlisle Canal	Meadows	06.55	
Haymarket 39	V2	20.50	Waverley Goods	Carlisle Canal	00.06	Class C goods
Haymarket 39	V2	01.30	Carlisle Canal	Niddrie West	04.32	01.30 Carlisle - Perth Class C Goods
St Margarets 51	B1	19.02	Edinburgh	Riccarton Jcn	21.48	Stopping Passenger
St Margarets 51	B1	21.55	Riccarton Jcn	Newcastleton	22.07	ECS
St Margarets 51	B1	22.30	Newcastleton	Carlisle	23.30	Light
St Margarets 51	B1	06.05	Carlisle	Niddrie West	10.33	Class D to Aberdeen
St Margarets 20	K3	02.20	Niddrie	Carlisle Canal	05.56	00.55 Inverkeithing - Carlisle. Class C
St Margarets 20	K3	08.00	Carlisle Canal	Niddrie West	12.37	Class D to Perth
St Margarets 21	K3	04.50	Niddrie	Carlisle Upperby	09.10	22.25 Aberdeen - Carlisle. Class C
St Margarets 21	K3	11.35	Carlisle Canal	Niddrie West	16.46	Class E to Aberdeen
St Margarets 22	K3	07.30	Niddrie	Carlisle Canal	12.14	00.30 Dundee West - Carlisle. Class E
St Margarets 22	K3	14.35	Carlisle Canal	Meadows	20.25	Class E
St Margarets 23	K3	11.00	Niddrie	Carlisle Canal	16.04	01.00 Aberdeen - Carlisle. Class E
St Margarets 23	K3	17.50	Carlisle Canal	Niddrie West	23.33	Class E to Aberdeen
St Margarets 24	K3	13.30	Niddrie	Carlisle Canal	18.39	Class E
St Margarets 24	K3	20.45	Carlisle Canal	Niddrie West	01.19	Class E
St Margarets 25	K3	14.55	Niddrie	Carlisle Canal	20.26	Class E
St Margarets 25	K3	22.00	Carlisle Canal	Portobello	04.02	Class E
Carlisle (Canal) 1A	A3	01.10	Canal	Niddrie West	04.12	Class C: Canal - Dundee goods
Carlisle (Canal) 1A	A3	08.35	Corstorphine	Edinburgh	08.48	
Carlisle (Canal) 1A	A3	10.05	Edinburgh	Carlisle	12.48	10.05 Edinburgh - St Pancras
Carlisle (Canal) 1A	A3	16.45	Carlisle	Edinburgh	19.22	08.50 Kings Cross - Edinburgh
Carlisle (Canal) 1B	A3	00.30	Haymarket Goods	Carlisle Canal	04.04	22.05 Dundee West - Carlisle Class C Goods
Carlisle (Canal) 1B	A3	13.26	Carlisle	Edinburgh	16.20	
Carlisle (Canal) 1B	A3	21.53	Edinburgh	Carlisle	00.26	21.53 Edinburgh - St Pancras
Carlisle (Canal) 1C	A3	09.05	Carlisle	Edinburgh	12.20	Stopping train
Carlisle (Canal) 1C	A3	17.53	Edinburgh	Carlisle	20.40	Works 1A
Carlisle (Canal) 10	K3	04.20	Carlisle Canal	Portobello	09.29	Class E
Carlisle (Canal) 10	K3	10.30	Portobello	Carlisle Canal	15.36	Class E
Carlisle (Canal) 11	K3	10.40	Carlisle Canal	Niddrie West	10.33	Class D to Aberdeen
Carlisle (Canal) 11	K3	16.35	Niddrie	Carlisle Canal	21.29	Class E
Carlisle (Canal) 12	K3	13.35	Carlisle Canal	Niddrie West	18.39	Class E
Carlisle (Canal) 12	K3	19.27	Portobello	Carlisle Canal	02.04	Class E
Carlisle (Canal) 13	K3	16.00	Carlisle Canal	Niddrie West	21.50	Class H
Carlisle (Canal) 13	K3	01.45	Niddrie	Carlisle Canal	05.19	20.20 Aberdeen - Carlisle. Class C

EDINBURGH - PEEBLES - GALASHIELS (1953)

m.ch	Class	K	K	Pass	Pass	Pass	K	K	K	K	K	K	Pass	Pass	Pass	K	Pass	Pass	Pass	K	Pass
	Train From	06.00 H'green						09.20 Peebles	09.20 Peebles	09.20 Peebles	09.20 Peebles										
	Engine	J36	J36	V1	V1	V1	J36	J36	J36	J36	J36	J36	V1	V1	V1	J36	V1	V1	V1	J36	V1
	Rep No.	695	695	340	342	344	520	520	520	520	520	751	346	348	350	756	354	356	358	578	364
0.00	EDINBURGH (W)			07.10	07.35	07.56							12.42	13.18	13.37		17.05	17.27	18.26		22.30
3.00	Portobello			07.19	07.43	08.02							12.48	13/24	13.46		17.11	17.36	18.32		22.36
4.33	Niddrie S. Jcn			07/22	07/41	08/05							12/51	13/27	13/49		17/13	17/39	18/35		22/39
6.19	Millerhill Jcn			07.25														17.42			
7.76	Eskbank			07.30	07.52	08.11							12.57	13.33	13.57		17.19	17.47	18.41		22.45
8.21	Hardengreen Jcn	06.00		07/31	07/53	08/12						08.35	12/58	13/34	13/58	14.10	17/20	17/48	18/42	19.00	22/46
8.59	Esk Valley Jcn			07/32	07/54	08/13							12/59	13/35	13/59	14/16	17/21	17/49	18/43		22/47
9.31	Bonnyrigg			_07.35_	07.57	08.16							13.02	13.38	14.02		17.24	17.52	_18.46_		22.49
11.15	**ROSEWELL**				08.02	08.22						08.56	13.07	13.43	14.07	14.25	17.29	17.57		19.19	
11.15	**ROSEWELL**					08.26						09.05		13.45		14.55	17.30			19.25	
12.46	Rosslynlee					08.30						(To		13.50		(To	17.34				
15.06	Pomathorn Halt					08.36						Peni-		13.57		Peni-	17.40				
17.41	**Leadburn Jcn**	06.30				08.41						cuik)				cuik)	17.45			19.59	
17.41	**Leadburn Jcn**	07.00				08.42								14/02			17.46			20.06	
22.71	Eddleston	07.15	07.30			08.52											17.56				
27.09	**PEEBLES**		07.40			08.59								14.17			18.03			20.38	
27.09	**PEEBLES**					09.02	09.20							14.19			18.05				
28.44	Peebles Gas Works						09.25	09.35													
30.30	Cardrona					09.10		09.40	09.50								18.11				
33.35	**Innerleithen**					09.16		09.57	09.57					14.30			18.16				
33.35	**Innerleithen**					09.17			10.53					14.31			18.17				
35.25	Walkerburn					09.21			10.58	11.05				14.35			18.21				
42.24	Clovenfords					09.33				11.20	11.28			14.47							
44.44	Kilnknowe Jcn					09/38					11/35			14/52			18/37				
45.47	**GALASHIELS**					09.40					11.40			14.54			18.39				

m.ch	Class	Pass	Pass	Pass	Pass	Pass	Pass	K	K	K	K	Pass	K	K	K	K	Pass	K	K	K	K
	Train From							11.00 Peebles	11.00 Peebles	11.00 Peebles			12.14 G'shiels	12.14 G'shiels	12.14 G'shiels			15.00 Peebles	15.00 Peebles	15.00 Peebles	
	Engine	V1	V1	V1	V1	V1	V1	J36	J36	J36	J36	V1	J36	J36	J36	J36	V1	J36	J36	J36	J36
	Rep No.	405	379	482	216	389	222	695	695	695	695	411	574	574	574	574	413	776	776	776	776
0.00	**GALASHIELS**				07.13	10.16						12.15									
1.03	Kilnknowe Jcn				07/15	10/18						12/20									
3.23	Clovenfords					10.24						12.25	12.30								
10.22	Walkerburn				07.31	10.36							13.00	13.05							
12.12	**Innerleithen**				07.35	10.40								13.11							
12.12	**Innerleithen**				07.36	10.41								13.30							
15.17	Cardrona					10.47								13.35	13.45						
18.38	**PEEBLES**				07.47	10.53									13.55						
18.38	**PEEBLES**				07.49	10.55		11.00										15.00			
22.56	Eddleston				07.57			11.10	11.15									15.15	15.30		
28.06	**Leadburn Jcn**				08.09				11.25										15.42		
28.06	**Leadburn Jcn**				08.10		11/13		11.30										15.52		
30.41	Pomathorn Halt				08.15				11.35	11.40											
32.31	Holme Bank Sdg																			16.00	16.10
33.01	Rosslynlee				08.20		11.22			11.50	12.00									16.15	16.20
34.32	**ROSEWELL**				08.23		11.25				12.05										16.29
34.32	**ROSEWELL**		07.41		08.25	08.48	11.26					13.37					15.32	16.50			16.50
36.16	Bonnyrigg	06.57	07.45		08.29	08.52	11.30					13.42					15.36	16.55			16.55
36.68	Esk Valley Jcn			08/04								13/43									
37.26	Hardengreen Jcn	06/59	07/47	08/05	08/32	08/54	11/32					13/44					15/38				
37.51	Eskbank	07.01	07.49	08.07	08.34	08.56	11.34					13.46					15.40				
39.28	Millerhill Jcn	07.05	07.53	08/10	08/38	08/59	11/37					13.50					15/43				
41.14	Niddrie S. Jcn	07/08	07/56	08/12	08/40	09/01	11/39					13/53					15/45				
42.47	Portobello	07.11	07.59	08.15	08.43	09.04	11.42					13.56					15.48				
45.47	**EDINBURGH (W)**	07.21	08.08	08.23	08.49	09.10	11.48					14.06					15.57				

m.ch	Class	K	Pass	Pass	Pass
	Train From	15.00 Peebles			
	Engine	J36	V1	V1	V1
	Rep No.	776	246	419	275
0.00	**GALASHIELS**		16.06		19.10
1.03	Kilnknowe Jcn		16/08		19/12
3.23	Clovenfords		16.14		
10.22	Walkerburn		16.26		19.28
12.12	**Innerleithen**		16.30		19.32
12.12	**Innerleithen**		16.31		19.33
15.17	Cardrona		16.37		
18.38	**PEEBLES**		16.43		19.44
18.38	**PEEBLES**		16.45		19.45
22.56	Eddleston		16.53		
28.06	**Leadburn Jcn**		17.04		
28.06	**Leadburn Jcn**		17.05		20/03
30.41	Pomathorn Halt		17.10		
32.31	Holme Bank Sdg				
33.01	Rosslynlee		17.15		
34.32	**ROSEWELL**		17.18		20.14
34.32	**ROSEWELL**		17.19		20.15
36.16	Bonnyrigg	17.01	17.23	19.30	20.19
36.68	Esk Valley Jcn				
37.26	Hardengreen Jcn	_17.08_	17/25	19/32	20/21
37.51	Eskbank		17.27	19.34	20.23
39.28	Millerhill Jcn		17.31		
41.14	Niddrie S. Jcn		17/34	19/39	20/28
42.47	Portobello		17.38	19.42	20.31
45.47	**EDINBURGH (W)**		17.49	19.48	20.37

By constructing the main line to take the most direct route between Edinburgh and Galashiels, the relatively important town of Peebles, twenty miles to the west of Galashiels, found itself in danger of missing the railway age; a fear that resulted in the construction of a line in 1855 that linked Hardengreen Junction with Peebles and extended eastwards to rejoin the main line at Kilnknowe Junction, a mile north of Galashiels. The resulting loop was absorbed by the North British in 1876 and although in pre-1914 days the northern end of the line saw a reasonable level of business, thanks mainly to the branch that diverged at Rosewell to Penicuik, passenger traffic over the remainder was infrequent and comprised only five trains between Edinburgh and Galashiels plus a connection from Peebles into the morning St Pancras train. Theoretically the line played a role as a diversionary route in the event of a major blockage on the main line between Hardengreen and Kilnknowe but the single-line operation of the loop south of Rosewell plus the fact it could not take any engine larger than a K3 made diversions awkward to arrange at short notice.

The Penicuik branch closed to passenger traffic in 1950, its services being reduced to a handful of rush-hour workings that turned round at either Rosewell or Bonnyrigg while Galashiels services continued to give the impression of being rationed with three trains from Edinburgh and four from Galashiels. (The imbalance arose from the fact that one of the workings ran outward via Falahill).

Goods and mineral traffic ran at a reasonably healthy level with three booked services starting from Hardengreen and two from Peebles. Trips were also run at the Controller's discretion between Hardengreen Yard and Whitehill colliery. Rosewell. J36 0-6-0's tended to be used for the goods services whilst St Margaret's V3 2-6-2T's worked the passenger duties. Locomotive facilities were provided at Peebles where a St Margaret's 0-6-0 recessed overnight. The engine's working started at Galashiels with the mid-day goods to Peebles before continuing with the 15.00 to Hardengreen and the 19.00 back to Peebles. The 0-6-0 then spent the night at Peebles shed before finishing the diagram with the 09.20 morning goods to Galashiels.

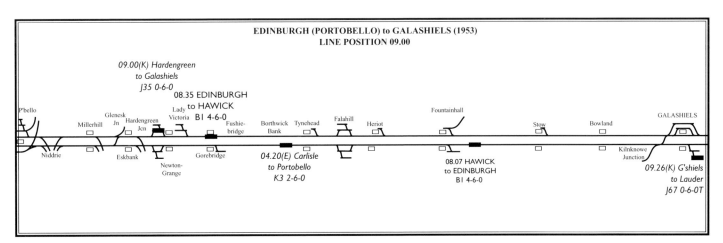

EDINBURGH (PORTOBELLO) to GALASHIELS (1953)
LINE POSITION 09.00

09.00(K) Hardengreen to Galashiels J35 0-6-0

08.35 EDINBURGH to HAWICK B1 4-6-0

04.20(E) Carlisle to Portobello K3 2-6-0

08.07 HAWICK to EDINBURGH B1 4-6-0

09.26(K) G'shiels to Lauder J67 0-6-0T

P'bello — Millerhill — Glenesk Jn — Hardengreen Jcn — Lady Victoria — Fushiebridge — Borthwick Bank — Tynehead — Falahill — Heriot — Fountainhall — Stow — Bowland — GALASHIELS

Niddrie — Eskbank — Newton-Grange — Gorebridge — Kilnknowe Junction

CONTROLLER'S LOG: Waverley route trains come in a variety of shapes, sizes and speeds but none is so remarkable as the Lauder goods which is being put together in Galashiels yard. Its unique feature is the tender-fitted J67 (Great Eastern!) 0-6-0 tank that works the service: this being the only class permitted over the 10-mile Fountainhall - Lauder branch which was built to light railway standards. The lightly laid branch posed considerable motive power problems for the North British and when the D51 4-4-0T's which worked many of the branches around Galashiels and Hawick were

At the present time efforts are in hand to find a suitable replacement for the two J67's at Galashiels - 68492 and 68511 - and some sleight of hand is taking place as a result. The axle-limit of the branch is 12 tons but someone has discovered that the weight of the new LMS 2MT 2-6-0's divided by four axles comes to 11.75 tons and on the basis of this (rather dubious) argument, 46461 has been used on occasions when neither J67 is available. (Since 46461 provides all-round protection from the weather, the incidence of J67 failures has increased of late).

services at Hawick within half an hour of each other gives some idea of the industrial activity that takes place in the Dundee area and one might have expected that services from Dundee to Carlisle would have run over the Caledonian via Kinbuck and Beattock. As it happens all three services from Dundee West run over the North British; two reversing at Buckingham Junction and running via Leuchars Junction and Burntisland with the third running via Perth, Glanfarg and Edinburgh. The Caledonian main line tends to be reserved for traffic travelling from the Glasgow and Motherwell

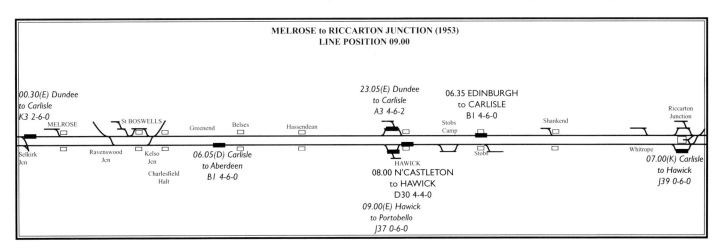

MELROSE to RICCARTON JUNCTION (1953)
LINE POSITION 09.00

00.30(E) Dundee to Carlisle K3 2-6-0

23.05(E) Dundee to Carlisle A3 4-6-2

06.35 EDINBURGH to CARLISLE B1 4-6-0

06.05(D) Carlisle to Aberdeen B1 4-6-0

08.00 N'CASTLETON to HAWICK D30 4-4-0

09.00(E) Hawick to Portobello J37 0-6-0

07.00(K) Carlisle to Hawick J39 0-6-0

MELROSE — St BOSWELLS — Greenend — Belses — Hassendean — Stobs Camp — Shankend — Riccarton Junction

Selkirk Jcn — Ravenswood Jcn — Kelso Jcn — Charlesfield Halt — HAWICK — Stobs — Whitrope

withdrawn, the LNER had to reach out as far as East Anglia for replacements which arrived in the shape of Great Eastern F7 2-4-2T's; the only engines of adequate axleweight that could be spared. The 2-4-2T's lasted until 1944 when - against considerable odds - they were replaced by another import from the Great Eastern, J67 0-6-0T's. Whilst meeting the axleweight criteria of the light railway, the J67's had insufficient coal and water capacity for the three and a half hour working and were therefore equipped with tenders; the only tank engines to be so altered.

The 23.05 ex Dundee and the 06.05 Carlisle - Aberdeen have exchanged crews at Hawick and the A3 of the former is ready - with its J36 banker in rear - to get away as soon as the 06.35 up passenger has left Stobs. Punctual running of the passenger is important since the last thing the 23.05 Dundee needs is a signal check on the climb up to Whitrope: the A3 will produce fireworks enough in the course of the climb without the added complication of having to restart its train on a 1 in 80 gradient.

The presence of two Dundee - Carlisle

areas and the only through working from the Northern section of the Caledonian to Carlisle or beyond is the overnight working from Inverness to Kingmoor. Aberdeen traffic is also routed over the North British via Edinburgh and the Waverley route.

One can see the evidence of this at this moment on the main line where a Carlisle to Aberdeen service is approaching St Boswells whilst a Carlisle - Perth train is grinding its way - K3 on the front and J39 in rear - up the 1 in 85 between Newcastleton and Steele Road.

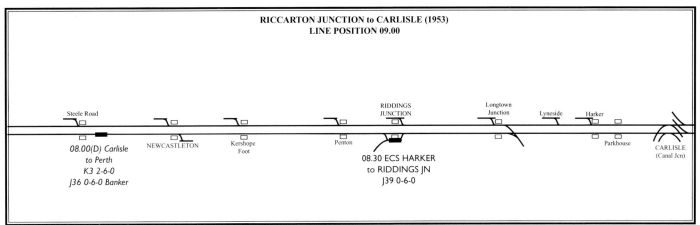

RICCARTON JUNCTION to CARLISLE (1953)
LINE POSITION 09.00

08.00(D) Carlisle to Perth K3 2-6-0 J36 0-6-0 Banker

08.30 ECS HARKER to RIDDINGS JN J39 0-6-0

Steele Road — RIDDINGS JUNCTION — Longtown Junction — Lyneside — Harker

Newcastleton — Kershope Foot — Penton — Parkhouse — CARLISLE (Canal Jcn)

The presence of V2 60973 will doubtless gladden the hearts of Carlisle enthusiasts since it had long been an Aberdeen engine and therefore seldom seen south of Perth.   In June 1960 - a month before the photograph was taken - it was transferred to Perth and its visits to Edinburgh became more frequent.   On one of these visits it had to be taken off diagram by the authorities at Edinburgh and placed into a Haymarket A3 diagram to work the 14.33 Edinburgh to Carlisle.   The train is seen passing under the Lothian lines at Niddrie North Junction.   The lines in the left foreground are the commencement of the Edinburgh Suburban lines which ran to the Waverley via Morningside Road and Haymarket.   The passenger service on the Suburban line was withdrawn in September 1962 and had consisted of eight 'circular' trains most of which ran during the rush hours.   Goods traffic over the suburban line was considerable.

The mid-day Edinburgh - Carlisle express passes Niddrie South Junction on 1st June 1961 behind Haymarket A1 Pacific 'Bonnie Dundee'.   These engines were not normally associated with the Waverley route but by the early 1960's the advance of dieselisation was such that they were liable for any Edinburgh-based work that became available.   Before the war this had been a through service to St Pancras and included a Pullman dining car as far as Carlisle but latterly it ran as a connection into the 13.30 Glasgow Central - Euston 'Mid-day Scot'.   (W.S.Sellar)

Glenesk Junction, Eskbank, was the point of divergence for the Dalkeith branch which lost its passenger service in January 1942. Goods services remained until the 1960's and were worked by one of the Hardengreen pilots which made two trips daily to and from Dalkeith. J35 0-6-0 64479 of St Margarets rejoins the main line with the 18.40 Dalkeith - Hardengreen Junction (engine and brake) trip on 21 April 1960. (W.S.Sellar)

In the days when it had a passenger service, Dalkeith probably held the distinction of having the longest gap between trains of any station in the country: sixteen hours (and four minutes) elapsing between the 21.18 departure and the 13.22 the following day. The object of this was to reduce the staffing of the station to a single (late-turn) shift and there cannot have been many scheduled services that lacked a morning train. The passenger service was withdrawn in 1942 leaving only a goods link with Hardengreen Junction. J35 64479 shunts the yard after arriving with the 08.45 from Hardengreen. (W.S.Sellar)

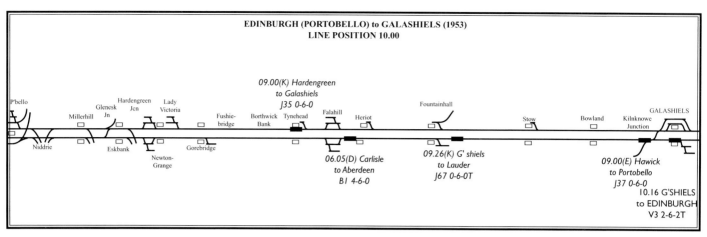

EDINBURGH (PORTOBELLO) to GALASHIELS (1953)
LINE POSITION 10.00

CONTROLLER'S LOG: Now is the time to take stock of traffic at the local stations and to determine whether or not the booked service will cope. The popular notion of a 'pick-up goods' working its way through every yard and station from Edinburgh to Carlisle does not apply - the route is far too long for such a thing - and instead there are a series of trip workings which between them cover most of the line.

Traffic and empty wagons for the Edinburgh-based service are tripped in overnight from Niddrie, Haymarket, Meadows and the other Edinburgh yards to Hardengreen Junction where they are made up into the 09.00 local to

to work all yards between Longtown Junction and Hawick and is supported by Target 21 which serves all points between Carlisle and Riccarton Junction. The latter is unusual in that it is worked by a D30 4-4-0 - the engine off the 07.12 Riccarton Junction to Carlisle passenger - rather than the usual J39 0-6-0.

Target 13 has been working its way steadily down the line for the past three hours and has reached Stobs. In a short while it will terminate at Hawick and then start back for Carlisle. In common with the Hardengreen trip the crew are on a bonus and will stay no longer than is absolutely necessary in Hawick.

The Thames-Forth may not be the fastest way of getting from Edinburgh to London but it is without question the most scenic and more often than not every seat in the train is taken. One sometimes wishes however that a different type of engine might be booked to the train.

On the through goods side of affairs, the slow progress of the 23.05 ex Dundee is noted as its Pacific and banker conclude an hour of uninterrupted climbing. Ten miles in rear the 00.30 Dundee - Carlisle changes crews with the 08.00 Carlisle - Perth and waits for a banker to buffer up to the brake.

At the southern end of the parish a pair of

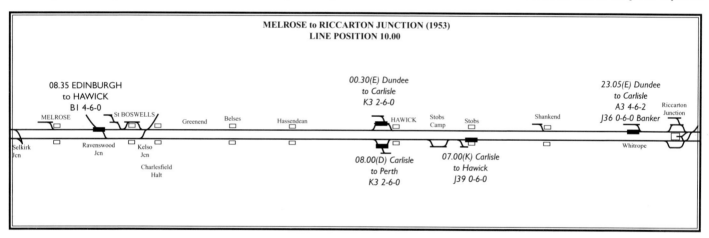

MELROSE to RICCARTON JUNCTION (1953)
LINE POSITION 10.00

Galashiels which calls at all intermediate points before turning at Galashiels and repeating the process in reverse. Its timings are for guidance rather than strict working purposes and to aid progress the crew are paid a bonus if they complete the fifty-mile round trip in good time. (For years this LNER scheme was held up to ridicule since it proved conclusively that workings such as the Galashiels trip could run to timings that were said to be impossible).

The southern end of the line is looked after by Target 13 which leaves Canal Yard at 07.00

The plateau between Hawick and Galashiels is not served by trip workings and stations such as St Boswells are dealt with by main line services.

From the look of the train board, the 09.00 ex Hardengreen - the prosaically named '551' - appears to have most of the line to itself but appearances can deceive since the star turn of the route - the London-bound 'Thames-Forth Express' - is on the point of leaving Edinburgh and a decision will have to be made as to where it is to overtake 551.

stopping trains pass each other; one worked by a B1 4-6-0 - a class of engine relatively uncommon south of Hawick - and the other by an A3 Pacific: the engine which worked up with last night's St Pancras sleeper.

The Pacific is followed by the strange sight of Target 21 as it ambles north behind the D30 4-4-0 which arrived in Carlisle with the 07.12 passenger Riccarton. It is booked to serve Longtown Junction, Riddings Junction and Newcastleton but can be used to service any of the other yards south of Riccarton Junction.

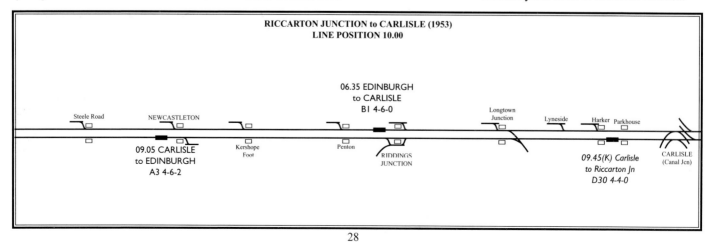

RICCARTON JUNCTION to CARLISLE (1953)
LINE POSITION 10.00

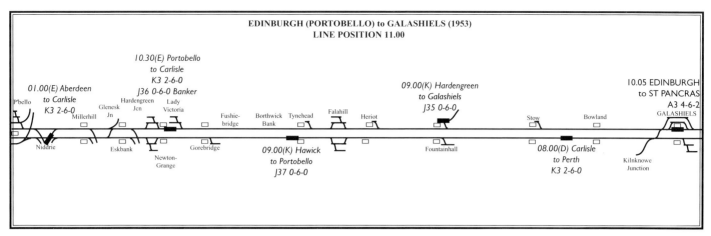

CONTROLLER'S LOG : The Thames - Forth express - which officially lost its name in 1939 - has managed to cover the first thirty-three miles of its journey without distress and is sitting at Galashiels ready to run the easily graded section to Hawick during which time the fireman will have an opportunity to get the engine ready for the 1 in 89 slog from Hawick to Whitrope.

Punctual running by the Midland Anglo-Scottish expresses is not something that can be taken for granted and five minutes dropped between Gorebridge and Falahill with a similar

of the name. The double-figure gradients of Falahill and Whitrope banks belonged to a different world and when the Pacifics were first sent to the line in 1928 the trains were very much lighter - five to seven coaches was the norm - than they were to become during and after the war. The midday service from Edinburgh to London was in fact diagrammed for nothing more powerful than a D49 4-4-0.

A Pacific in good order is not by any means a risk-free proposition while an A3 with problems presents a number of difficulties since the ways in which assistance can be given are

Double-heading, the usual panacea for badly steaming engines, cannot be resorted to between Edinburgh and Carlisle since A3 locomotives cannot form part of a double-headed combination. (In this connection, if an express is going to perform badly, one prefers that the engine should be a B1 4-6-0 since at least it can be double-headed).

What would be useful would be an engine specific to the route and one wonders why the range of BR Standard engines does not included a type designed with the harder parts of Scotland in mind.

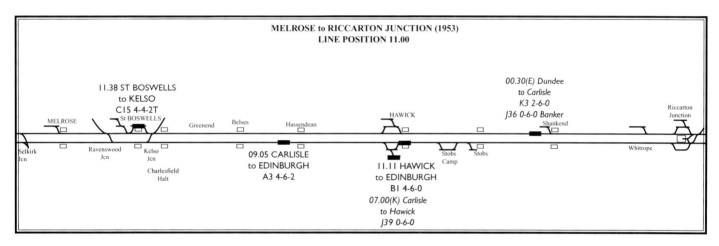

amount being lost from Hawick to Whitrope is typical rather than exceptional. The Thames-Forth is one of the few trains to be granted recovery time - two minutes between Hawick and Carlisle - in its schedule.

The problem lies not so much with the engines so much as the individual who decreed that an A3 Pacific was suited to the Waverley route. What he chose to ignore was the fact that the A3's were designed with the relatively flat contours of the East Coast line in mind: four hundred miles with scarcely a gradient worthy

more limited than they would be on another line. A banker can be used from Hardengreen to Falahill and from Hawick to Whitrope but it has to be coupled to the train with the vacuum hose connected and the time lost coupling and uncoupling is unlikely to be very different to that dropped by unassisted poor steaming. Another objection to assisting a passenger train to Falahill, Whitrope or both is that banking engines are finite in number and using one to help a Pacific could well strand a goods service for an hour or more.

In the opposite direction the Pacific-hauled 09.05 Carlisle - Edinburgh slow gets close to St Boswells and behind it a B1 backs a set of stock into Hawick to form the 11.11 to Edinburgh. In the adjacent yard the J39 0-6-0 that arrived half an hour ago with target 21 turns and prepares to return to Carlisle.

The presence of a C15 4-4-2T at St Boswells with the Thames-Forth's Kelso connection reminds one of pre-1939 days when the Kelso coaches arrived in St Boswells on the rear of the London train.

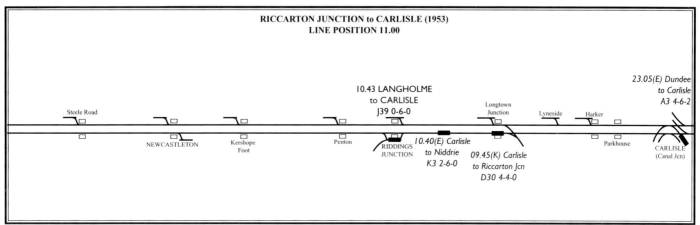

The principal passenger workings - and a handful of goods services - over the Waverley route were handled by six A3 Pacifics; three from Carlisle Canal and three from Edinburgh Haymarket. The class had been active on the route since 1928 but because of the severity of Whitrope and Falahill banks were not the ideal engines for the line. In prewar days trains did not normally exceed six or seven coaches and the A3's were able to cope without too much difficulty but in postwar days the loads of ten and more carriages became too much - the A3's had been designed for the level gradients of the East Coast route - and loss of time through slipping became commonplace. A scheme for through engine working between Edinburgh and Leeds was tried in early BR days but was very quickly abandoned. The problem was not resolved until the Pacifics came to be rebuilt with double blastpipes in the very late 1950's. Double-chimney A3 60094 'Colorado' of Haymarket shed passes Hardengreen with the 14.33 Edinburgh to Carlisle semi-fast on 21 April 1960. (W.S.Sellar)

With its sidings and banking duties, Hardengreen was one of the more important locations on the route and provided employmnent for no less than four J36 0-6-0's which banked goods services up the nine-mile climb to Falahill summit plus several J35 0-6-0's which covered the local trip workings. J35 64462 waits for its next duty at Hardengreen Junction. (W.S.Sellar)

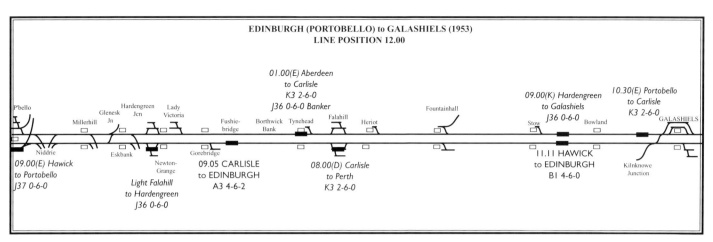

EDINBURGH (PORTOBELLO) to GALASHIELS (1953)
LINE POSITION 12.00

CONTROLLER'S LOG: *"- Whitrope. The Pullman's overtime."*

"- What time did you get it on line?"

"- Eleven fifty-seven and no sign of it."

"- Next down to you will be the 10.40 Carlisle goods. Don't offer it forward until you hear from me."

It is now 12.20 and the Carlisle Pacific of the 10.05 Edinburgh - St Pancras seems to be making heavy weather of the climb to Whitrope. It left Hawick on time at eleven thirty-seven and should have passed Stobs Camp at 11.43, Stobs at 11.46, Shankend at 11.53 and Whitrope at

" - Riccarton Junction? Hold the 10.40 Carlisle goods."

" - I'm all off for it and it's approaching my home signal."

" - Put on against it. Give it a red if you must but don't let it into the section until you hear from me."

The next call is to the Riccarton stationmaster to ask him to ride on the engine of the 10.40 Carlisle in order to take charge at Whitrope. The signalbox is instructed to let the goods down to Whitrope as soon as the SM is on the engine. The signalman tells you that

be done by a light engine whilst the presence of the SM is necessary because there is a tunnel between Whitrope and Shankend. If the engine gets to Shankend and reports the express a failure then the K3 can be crossed-over and sent in to assist in rear.

"- Goods away from Riccarton Junction at twelve twenty-seven. The SM's on the engine."

That means it should get to Whitrope by 12.34 and, after leaving its train pinned down on the down main, be away to examine the line by about 12 40 reaching Shankend with its report about five minutes later. While waiting, the

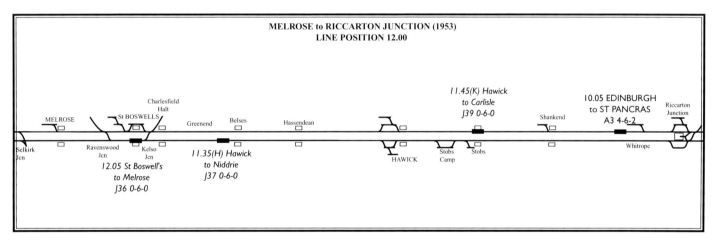

MELROSE to RICCARTON JUNCTION (1953)
LINE POSITION 12.00

12.03. The engine dropped four minutes to Shankend - which is not unusual - but nothing has been heard of it since. The Shankend - Whitrope section is a four miles stretch of 1 in 81 and an express would normally need ten minutes to cover it. At the moment there is no clue as to whether the train is simple struggling, has come to a stand or is even on its side blocking the opposite line. Until a member of its crew materialises, the 10.40 Carlisle - Niddrie goods will have to wait at Whitrope since we cannot be sure the line is clear.

the driver doubts if he can restart the train on the bank: the 10.40 is one of the few not to take a banker.

"- Put the pilot on the rear and tell it to bank to Whitrope."

The plan is to use the K3 a to examine the line between Whitrope and Shankend and to find out where - and what has happened - to the express. Therefore when the 10.40 gets to Whitrope and if there is still no sign of the express, the K3 will be detached to run forward to examine the line as far as Shankend - something that can only

news that the London is running at least half an hour late is relayed to the Carlisle Controller.

" - Whitrope here. I can hear the London coming towards me. Some way off and going very slow....."

At least we know where the thing is and that it is still on the move.

" - Goods arrived at Whitrope 'thirty-four. Up express passed at thirty five, picking up speed."

Another instance of the wrong type of engine for the route....

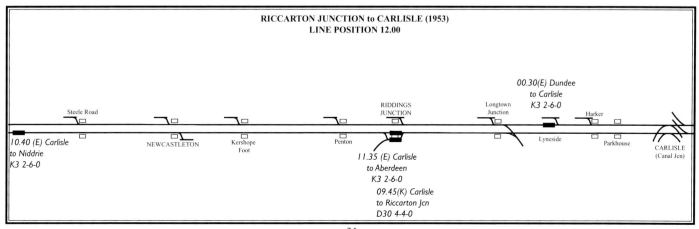

RICCARTON JUNCTION to CARLISLE (1953)
LINE POSITION 12.00

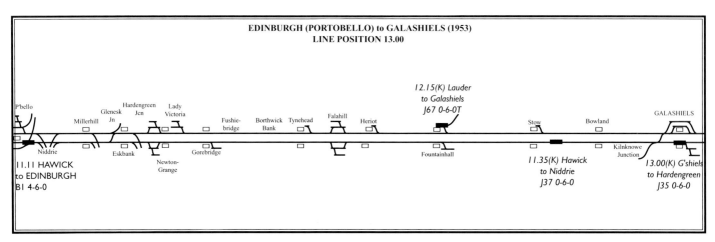

EDINBURGH (PORTOBELLO) to GALASHIELS (1953)
LINE POSITION 13.00

CONTROLLER'S LOG: After the excitement (sic) of the Thames-Forth the tension relaxes and the atmosphere becomes less charged. A couple of through goods trains swap crews at Hawick whilst a pair of Carlisle - Aberdeen services pass Riccarton Junction and St Boswells respectively, their crews getting ready to changeover when they reach Hawick in about an hour's time. The up working has been shunted to allow the 12.05 Edinburgh - Carlisle express pass.

This last-mentioned is another A3 working but, the train consisting of only half a dozen bogies, is unlikely to run into problems on either far as Carlisle. The London section consisted of only one coach which was attached to a St Enoch - St Pancras express and the remainder returned to Edinburgh with the 18.29 (12.00 ex St Pancras) from Carlisle. The lightweight nature of the service was reflected in the engine diagram which called only for a Haymarket D49 4-4-0.

One thing that enthusiasts travelling on the 12.05 will be on the look-out for on passing Fountainhall is a sighting of the Lauder trip and - unless 46461 is in the working - its tender-fitted Great Eastern J67 0-6-0T. Unfortunately there is no guarantee of luck since the express dry mouth and an overfull ashtray. One often finds, for example, that an excess of last-minute traffic means that 108 trip (11.45 Hawick to Carlisle) will have a full load by the time it gets to Riddings Junction and cannot therefore work the stations to the south. One can try and find an engine, men and brakevan at Riccarton Junction (some hope at short notice) or run 108 fast to Carlisle and tempt the crew with overtime to return to Riddings Junction for the residue or relieve the engine at Canal and get it to do a second trip. There always seems to be more traffic than there are trains - especially the trip workings. In the meantime one has to

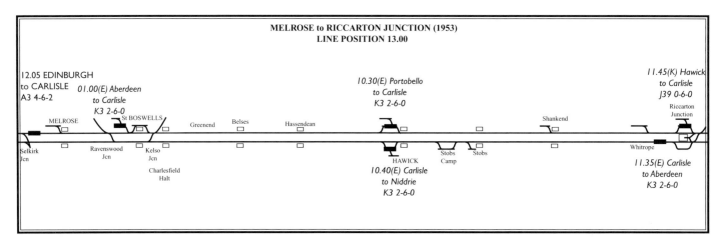

MELROSE to RICCARTON JUNCTION (1953)
LINE POSITION 13.00

Falahill or Whitrope. The engine diagram for this particular turn illustrates the wide variety of trains worked by A3's across the border since earlier in the day the same engine worked the 00.10 Carlisle - Niddrie class E goods and will later return to Edinburgh with the 19.44 stopping train from Carlisle.

The 12.05 is occasionally referred to as 'The Pullman' since it ran through to St Pancras before the war and included in its four-coach formation a Pullman car which served meals as is booked through Fountainhall twenty minutes before the trip is due to arrive but it is not unknown for the J67 to run early and be running round its train as the 12.05 passes through.

Most of the current workload is created by the various trip services that can be seen at Galashiels, Riccarton Junction and Steele Road. Arrangements for each service have to be made and confirmed with every yard the trains call at as they proceed along the line and the degree of extemporisation leaves one with a calculate the best place - probably Kershopefoot - for it to shunt for the 12.05 express.

The amount of work done by the trips can be gauged by the progress of the 09.45 Carlisle - Riccarton Junction which has served most points from Carlisle yet in spite of having been over three hours on the road has barely reached Steele Road. For the moment it shares the novelty of being worked by a D30 4-4-0 and having the entire route south of Riccarton Junction to itself.

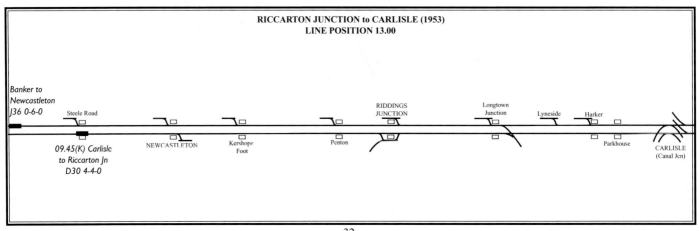

RICCARTON JUNCTION to CARLISLE (1953)
LINE POSITION 13.00

The A3 Pacifics and the Waverley route had an association that lasted more than thirty years although the relationship became a little strained at times during the postwar years as the class struggled to keep time with increasingly heavy trains on Falahill and Whitrope banks. The North British engine workings were self-contained and the A3's worked only to Carlisle where they handed the Anglo-Scottish trains over to LMS 5XP 4-6-0's for the run to Leeds City. By a twist of irony when A3 Pacifics were allocated to the companion St Pancras - Glasgow (St Enoch) services in 1960, they worked through from Leeds to Glasgow while the Edinburgh services retained their change of engine at Carlisle until dieselisation. (This did not prevent an almost ritual request from the Carlisle Controller to his opposite number at Edinburgh to ensure that the Thames-Forth Pacific rang off Haymarket loco with enough coal to work to Leeds!) The 10.05 'Waverley' from Edinburgh to London (St Pancras) is seen at Gorebridge during the summer of 1959 on the ascent of Falahill behind 60068 'Sir Visto' and 60079 'Bayardo', both of Carlisle (Canal). Both engines have been 'coaled for Leeds' and the relaxed attitude of the fireman on 60079 speaks well of the steaming qualities of the A3's after the fitting of double-chimneys - an enhancement that resolved most of the former difficulties with the class. (W.S.Sellar)

One can understand why some of the more remote stations on the line received a very infrequent service but it might have been expected that Gorebridge - the first station on the line and only twelve miles from the heart of Edinburgh - would have been included in the suburban arrangements. In fact Gorebridge was served by the irregular Edinburgh - Hawick or Galashiels trains and the only concession made to its proximity was the running of the V3-hauled 13.03 Edinburgh to Gorebridge in order to fill the gap between the 08.35 and 16.10 Edinburgh to Hawick trains. The 13.03 also ran on Saturdays and with the preceding 12.52 (SO) Edinburgh - Hawick gave Gorebridge the unusual experience of receiving two trains within a quarter of an hour of each other. The 12.52 was diagrammed to a Hawick 4-4-0 but by 1959 the supply of suitable engines had become so acute - all five D30 4-4-0's had been withdrawn without replacement - that St Margarets was obliged to send D49 62715 'Roxburghshire' to Hawick for its last few weeks of service. On 9th May 1959 it is seen arriving at Gorebridge with the 12.52 ex Edinburgh and (below) the same engine prepares to leave Gorebridge, two weeks later, with the return working, the 14.08 to Edinburgh. (W.S.Sellar)

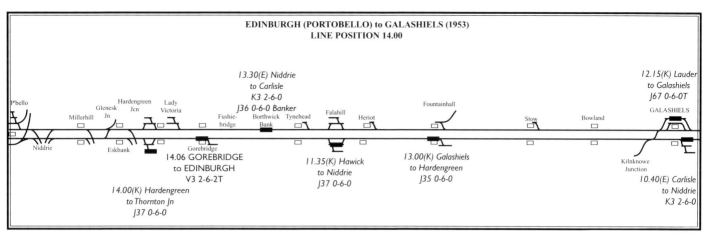

EDINBURGH (PORTOBELLO) to GALASHIELS (1953)
LINE POSITION 14.00

13.30(E) Niddrie to Carlisle K3 2-6-0
J36 0-6-0 Banker
12.15(K) Lauder to Galashiels J67 0-6-0T
14.06 GOREBRIDGE to EDINBURGH V3 2-6-2T
11.35(K) Hawick to Niddrie J37 0-6-0
13.00(K) Galashiels to Hardengreen J35 0-6-0
10.40(E) Carlisle to Niddrie K3 2-6-0
14.00(K) Hardengreen to Thornton Jn J37 0-6-0

CONTROLLER'S LOG: A number of interesting engines have appeared, making a change from the A3's and K3's that work the principal through trains.

Suburban trains are seldom seen on the Waverley line and the V3 2-6-2T's which power most of the Edinburgh Suburban services are as good as unknown over Falahill. One of the exceptions is the 13.03 Edinburgh to Gorebridge and its return service which is worked by one of St Margaret's fourteen 2-6-2T's and the only other appearance made by the class is on the 17.10 Edinburgh - Galashiels although several occasionally falls by the wayside, having to be rescued by a North Eastern engine. On more than one instance both Hawick engines have failed on two successive nights resulting in all Newcastle - Hawick services being worked by NER D49 4-4-0's for several days at a time. It is not unknown for St Margarets to send a D49 to Hawick - D11's are not unknown - to cover one of the Newcastle diagrams.

One of the workings in question, the 11.20 Newcastle to Hawick, is at Shankend. Provided it is fit to do so, the engine will work back to Tyneside with the 16.32 Hawick to hours; at 13.57. (Those who object to the Pullman supplement can follow in the 09.50 ex Newcastle and still be in London in under nine hours). The fastest time from Hawick to London however is by the 12.05 ex Edinburgh and the Midday Scot from Carlisle; the journey taking slightly less than seven and a half hours.

Another loco curiosity is 4MT 2-6-0 43139 which can be seen at Riddings Junction with the Langholm connection out of the 13.26 Carlisle - Edinburgh semi-fast. The 2-6-0 will work the remainder of the day's services on the Langholm branch, finishing with the 18.24

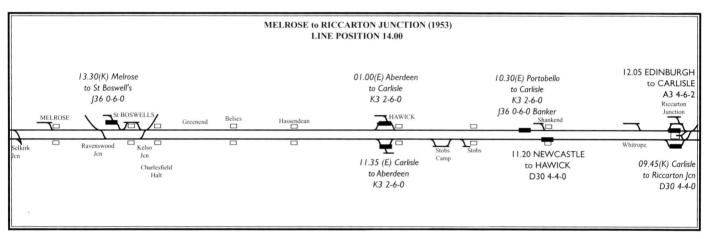

MELROSE to RICCARTON JUNCTION (1953)
LINE POSITION 14.00

13.30(K) Melrose to St Boswell's J36 0-6-0
01.00(E) Aberdeen to Carlisle K3 2-6-0
10.30(E) Portobello to Carlisle K3 2-6-0
J36 0-6-0 Banker
12.05 EDINBURGH to CARLISLE A3 4-6-2
11.35 (E) Carlisle to Aberdeen K3 2-6-0
11.20 NEWCASTLE to HAWICK D30 4-4-0
09.45(K) Carlisle to Riccarton Jcn D30 4-4-0

can be seen on the Galashiels services which runs over the Peebles route.

The purpose of the 13.03 is to give Gorebridge a service between the 08.35 and 16.10 departures from Edinburgh.

D49 4-4-0's were once familiar sights on the line but have had much of their work taken over by B1 4-6-0's and tend nowadays to be seen when deputising for shortages of power.

This often happens in the case of the Hawick - Newcastle workings which are booked to be covered by a pair of Hawick D30 4-4-0's, one of which stables overnight at Blaydon and Newcastle and spend the night on Heaton loco before returning with the 05.50 Newcastle - Riccarton Junction.

Very few passengers seem to take the Hawick - Newcastle trains seriously but they do in fact offer an additional route to London which compares favourably in terms of time to that of the Midland.

The through day service leaves Hawick at 11.37 and takes over nine hours to reach St Pancras yet by catching the 06.15 and travelling via Newcastle and the Tees-Tyne Pullman, one can reach London in seven and three-quarter Langholm - Carlisle.

The 13.26 from Carlisle is one of the Canal A3 diagrams and is the outward working of the 21.45 Edinburgh - St Pancras overnight sleeper. The service is part of a complex three-day cycle: yesterday the engine worked the down Thames Forth from Carlisle to Edinburgh and tomorrow - if it remains in diagram - it will cover the 09.05 Carlisle - Edinburgh and the 17.53 return service. The average daily mileage worked by these engines is not great - 260 miles - although account must be taken of the vertical as well as the horizontal distance travelled!

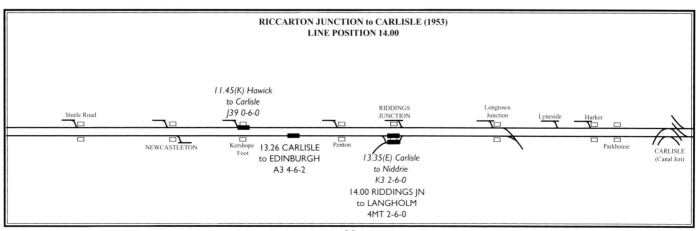

RICCARTON JUNCTION to CARLISLE (1953)
LINE POSITION 14.00

11.45(K) Hawick to Carlisle J39 0-6-0
13.26 CARLISLE to EDINBURGH A3 4-6-2
13.35(E) Carlisle to Niddrie K3 2-6-0
14.00 RIDDINGS JN to LANGHOLM 4MT 2-6-0

CARLISLE - SILLOTH (1955)

m. ch Class	K	Diesel	Diesel	K	K	K	K	K	Diesel	Diesel		Diesel	Diesel
Train	05.50			11.40	11.40	11.40	11.40	11.40					
From	Canal			Canal	Canal	Canal	Canal	Canal					
0.00 **CARLISLE**		09.20	11.20						13.22	15.45	16.48	18.20	21.00
1.27 Canal Junction	05/52	09/24	11/24	11/43					13/26	15/49	16/52	18/24	21/04
4.27 Kirkandrews		09.31	11.31	11.53	12.00				13.33	15.56	17.00	18.31	
6.22 Burgh-by-Sands		09.35	11.35		12.07	12.15			13.37	16.00	17.06	18.35	
9.35 **DRUMBURGH**	06.12	09.39	11.39			12.24			13.42	16.04	17.12	18.40	21.17
9.35 **DRUMBURGH**	06.16	09.40	11.40			12.28			13.43	16.05	17.13	18.41	21.18
12.64 Kirkbride	06.26	09.46	11.46			12.38	13.00		13.49	16.11	17.20	18.47	21.24
17.64 Abbeytown	06.39	09.54	11.54				13.11	13.20	13.56	16.19	17.30	18.54	21.31
20.18 Blackdyke Halt									14.01	16.23	17.35	18.59	
22.23 **SILLOTH**	06.50	10.01	12.01					13.30	14.05	16.28	17.40	19.03	21.38

m. ch Class	Diesel	Diesel	Diesel	K	K	K	K	Diesel	Pcls	Diesel	K	Diesel
Train				14.45	14.45	14.45						
From				Silloth	Silloth	Silloth						
0.00 **SILLOTH**	07.55	12.24	14.15	14.45				16.48	18.15	19.30	19.55	21.45
2.05 Blackdyke Halt	08.00	12.29						16.53				
4.39 Abbeytown	08.05	12.34	14.23	14.59	15.09			16.58	18.23	19.38	20/09	21.53
9.39 Kirkbride	08.13	12.42	14.31		15.25	15.37		17.06	18.33	19.46		
12.68 **DRUMBURGH**	08.17	12.46	14.35			15.48		17.11	18.39	19.50		22.04
12.68 **DRUMBURGH**	08.18	12.47	14.36			16.01		17.15	18.43	19.51	20/30	22.05
16.01 Burgh-by-Sands	08.24	12.53	14.42			16.11	16.18	17.21		19.57		
17.76 Abbeytown	08.29	12.58	14.47					17.26		20.02		
20.76 Canal Junction	08/35	13/04	14/53				16/35	17/32	18/56	20/08	20/55	22/18
22.23 **CARLISLE**	08.38	13.07	14.56					17.35	19.01	20.11		22.21
Destination						Canal					Canal	

RIDDINGS JUNCTION to LANGHOLME (1955)

m. ch Class	K	Pass	G	Pass	Pass
Train	05.25		Light		17.08
From	Canal		Canal		C'lisle
0.00 **RIDDINGS JCN**	06/07	10.04	11/40	14.00	17.38
1.29 Cononbie		10.09		14.05	17.43
2.62 Gilnockie		10.14		14.10	17.48
4.48 Glentorras					
7.08 **LANGHOLME**	06.35	10.23	12.00	14.19	17.57

m. ch	Mixed	Pass	K	Pass	Pass
0.00 **LANGHOLME**	07.13	10.42	12.45	15.30	18.24
2.40 Glentorras					
4.26 Gilnockie	07.24		13.15	15.39	18.33
5.59 Cononbie	07.30	10.54	13.25	15.44	18.38
7.08 **RIDDINGS JCN**	07.34	10.58	13.35	15.48	18.42
Destination		C'lisle		C'lisle	C'lisle

LONGTOWN to GRETNA : 1953

m. ch		H	H	H
Train		12.15	12.15	12.15
From		Canal	Canal	Canal
0.00 Longtown Jcn	12.40			
WD Sidings	12.50	13.05		
3.17 Gretna				
Moss Litter Sdgs				14.00
Blackbank Sdgs		13.20	14.10	

m. ch		H	H	H
Blackbank Sdgs	13.30	14.25		
Moss Litter Sdgs	13.40			
0.00 Gretna		14.35	15.00	
WD Sidings		15.20	15.50	
3.17 Longtown Jcn			16.00	
Destination			Canal	

A line upon which J39 0-6-0's predominated was the Silloth branch which branched from the Waverley route a mile north of Carlisle and followed the Cumberland coast for twenty miles before terminating in Silloth. The population of four thousand was served by seven passenger trains to and from Carlisle daily but the greater part of the lines' income came from the extensive harbour facilities - much of Silloth's traffic consisted of export coal to Northern Ireland - which were fed by two goods trains from Carlisle each day. This curious LNER outpost set deep in the heart of LNWR country lost much of its interest in late 1954 when diesel multiple-units took over the passenger service, leaving only the 16.48 Carlisle - Silloth and the 18.15 Silloth - Carlisle parcels to be steam-worked. Seasonal traffic to Silloth was at times considerable and the diesels were often overwhelmed with the result that steam workings had to be hurriedly reintroduced whenever heavy demand was anticipated. In the view above, J39 0-6-0 64932 couples up to the stock of the 14.40 Silloth to Carlisle on 16th June 1960 whilst sister-engine 64877 shunts the yard. The latter engine worked a long day at Silloth which started with the 05.50 Canal Yard to Silloth Goods and was followed by twelve hours shunting in Silloth yard before returning to Carlisle with the 19.55 goods. Somewhere out of sight is a third J39 0-6-0 which is waiting to leave with the 14.45 goods to Carlisle.

The seven-mile branch from Riddings Junction terminated at Langholme (pop 2400) and generated a service of five passenger trains to and from Riddings Junction or Carlisle plus a daily goods service.   Carlisle-based J39 0-6-0's were the usual engines provided for the branch services until 1951 when the afternoon working was diagrammed to 4MT 2-6-0 43139.   In the upper view J39 0-6-0 prepares to leave Langholm with the 10.42 to Carlisle, the last duty in its diagram which commenced with the 05.25 goods from Canal Yard and continued with two return passenger trips to and from Riddings Junction.   It's successor for the day was 43139 which came out light from Carlisle to work the 12.45 goods to Riddings Junction followed by a pair of Langholme - Carlisle passenger workings.   In the lower view J39 64733 has been substituted for 43139 and waits to leave Langholm on the 10th June 1960 with the 18.24 to Carlisle, the last train of the day.   The three departures of 1953 compared poorly with the seven of the 1930's; the four additional services - all of which ran through to Carlisle - being operated by a Sentinel railcar No. 39 'Protector'..

D49 4-4-0 62705 'Lanarkshire' of Haymarket arrives at Gorebridge with the 12.52 Edinburgh - Hawick on Saturday 23 May 1959. (W.S.Sellar)

Engine	Class	Aug-50	Sep-50	Oct-50	Nov-50	Dec-50	Jan-51	Feb-51	Mar-51	Apr-51	May-51	Jun-51	Jul-51
							LOCOMOTIVE ALLOCATION & MOVEMENTS : CARLISLE (CANAL) - 12B						
48074	8F 2-8-0 (1935)											To Willesden	X
48323	8F 2-8-0 (1935)											To Widnes	X
48544	8F 2-8-0 (1935)											To Bletchley	X
48708	8F 2-8-0 (1935)	X	X	X	X	X	X	X	X	X	X	Ex Widnes	
90063	8F : WD 2-8-0 (1943)				To Spital B	X	X	X	X	X	X	X	X
60068	7P: A3 4-6-2 (1922)												
60079	7P: A3 4-6-2 (1922)												
60093	7P: A3 4-6-2 (1922)												
60095	7P: A3 4-6-2 (1922)												
61851	6F: K3 2-6-0 (1924)												
61854	6F: K3 2-6-0 (1924)												
61858	6F: K3 2-6-0 (1924)												
61882	6F: K3 2-6-0 (1924)												
61898	6F: K3 2-6-0 (1924)												
61916	6F: K3 2-6-0 (1924)	X	X	X	X	X	X	X	X	X	X	X	Ex E'bro (SM)
61936	6F: K3 2-6-0 (1924)												
61937	6F: K3 2-6-0 (1924)												
61217	5MT: B1 4-6-0 (1942)												
61219	5MT: B1 4-6-0 (1942)												
61222	5MT: B1 4-6-0 (1942)												
45014	5MT 4-6-0 (1934)						To Longsight	X	X	X	X	X	X
45096	5MT 4-6-0 (1934)											To Preston	X
45454	5MT 4-6-0 (1934)											To Wigan (SB)	X
64727	5F: J39 0-6-0 (1926)	X	X	X	X	X	Ex H. Mersey						
64733	5F: J39 0-6-0 (1926)	X	X	X	X	X	Ex H. Mersey						
64875	5F: J39 0-6-0 (1926)												
64877	5F: J39 0-6-0 (1926)												
64880	5F: J39 0-6-0 (1926)												
64884	5F: J39 0-6-0 (1926)												
64888	5F: J39 0-6-0 (1926)												
64895	5F: J39 0-6-0 (1926)												
64899	5F: J39 0-6-0 (1926)							To Brunswick	X	X	X	X	X
64912	5F: J39 0-6-0 (1926)												
64930	5F: J39 0-6-0 (1926)												
64932	5F: J39 0-6-0 (1926)												
64948	5F: J39 0-6-0 (1926)												
64964	5F: J39 0-6-0 (1926)												
62730	4P: D49 4-4-0 (1927)		To Starbeck	X	X	X	X	X	X	X	X	X	X
62731	4P: D49 4-4-0 (1927)		To Starbeck	X	X	X	X	X	X	X	X	X	X
62732	4P: D49 4-4-0 (1927)		To Starbeck	X	X	X	X	X	X	X	X	X	Ex York
62734	4P: D49 4-4-0 (1927)		To Starbeck	X	X	X	X	X	X	X	X	X	Ex York
62735	4P: D49 4-4-0 (1927)		To Starbeck	X	X	X	X	X	X	X	X	X	X
40118	3P 2-6-2 (1935)	X	X	X	X	X	Ex T. Park						
69139	3F: N15 0-6-2T (1910)												
69155	3F: N15 0-6-2T (1910)												
69174	3F: N15 0-6-2T (1910)												
69185	3F: N15 0-6-2T (1910)												
69197	3F: N15 0-6-2T (1910)												
69215	3F: N15 0-6-2T (1910)												
69218	3F: N15 0-6-2T (1910)												
64478	3F: J35 0-6-0 (1906)												
64499	3F: J35 0-6-0 (1906)												
64511	3F: J35 0-6-0 (1906)												
64526	3F: J35 0-6-0 (1906)												
62281	2P: D31 4-4-0 (1890)												
67458	2P: C15 4-4-2T (1911)												
67474	2P: C15 4-4-2T (1911)												
67481	2P: C15 4-4-2T (1911)												
40673	2P 4-4-0 (1928)				To Upperby	X	X	X	X	X	X	X	X
68499	2F: J67 0-6-0T (1890)												
65216	2F: J36 0-6-0 (1888)												
65293	2F: J36 0-6-0 (1888)												
65304	2F: J36 0-6-0 (1888)												
65312	2F: J36 0-6-0 (1888)												
65321	2F: J36 0-6-0 (1888)												
12084	0F: Diesel 0-6-0	X	X	X	X	NEW		To Upperby	X	X	X	X	Ex Upperby
12085	0F: Diesel 0-6-0	X	X	X	X	NEW		To Upperby	X	X	X	X	Ex Upperby
12086	0F: Diesel 0-6-0	X	X	X	X	NEW		To Upperby	X	X	X	X	Ex Upperby
12087	0F: Diesel 0-6-0	X	X	X	X	NEW		To Upperby	X	X	X	X	X

The V1 2-6-2T's were one of the most successful classes of engine produced by the LNER, their only drawback being a rather limited water capacity which ruled them out of consideration for the Kings Cross suburban services. A considerable number of the class were allocated to Haymarket and St Margarets for the working of the Edinburgh suburban network which brought the class on a regular basis to Galashiels via Peebles. They were less frequently seen on the main line although one of the St Margarets engines was diagrammed to the 13.03 Edinburgh - Gorebridge and the 14.06 return working. 67624 of St Margarets pulls away from Gorebridge with the 14.06 to Edinburgh on 22 May 1959. (W.S.Sellar)

	LOCOMOTIVE ALLOCATION & MOVEMENTS : CARLISLE (CANAL) - 12B												
Engine	Class	Aug-51	Sep-51	Oct-51	Nov-51	Dec-51	Jan-52	Feb-52	Mar-52	Apr-52	May-52	Jun-52	Jul-52
48708	8F 2-8-0 (1935)											To Kingmoor	
60068	7P: A3 4-6-2 (1922)												
60079	7P: A3 4-6-2 (1922)												
60093	7P: A3 4-6-2 (1922)												
60095	7P: A3 4-6-2 (1922)												X
60111	7P: A3 4-6-2 (1922)												
61851	6F: K3 2-6-0 (1924)												
61854	6F: K3 2-6-0 (1924)												
61858	6F: K3 2-6-0 (1924)												
61882	6F: K3 2-6-0 (1924)												
61898	6F: K3 2-6-0 (1924)												
61916	6F: K3 2-6-0 (1924)												
61936	6F: K3 2-6-0 (1924)												
61937	6F: K3 2-6-0 (1924)												
61217	5MT: B1 4-6-0 (1942)												
61219	5MT: B1 4-6-0 (1942)												
61222	5MT: B1 4-6-0 (1942)												
61395	5MT: B1 4-6-0 (1942)	X	X	X	X	X	X	NEW					
44790	5MT 4-6-0 (1934)	X	X	X	X	X	X	X	X	X	Ex Polmadie		
44792	5MT 4-6-0 (1934)	X	X	X	X	X	X	X	X	X	Ex Polmadie		
64727	5F: J39 0-6-0 (1926)												
64733	5F: J39 0-6-0 (1926)												
64875	5F: J39 0-6-0 (1926)												
64877	5F: J39 0-6-0 (1926)												
64880	5F: J39 0-6-0 (1926)												
64884	5F: J39 0-6-0 (1926)												
64888	5F: J39 0-6-0 (1926)												
64895	5F: J39 0-6-0 (1926)												
64899	5F: J39 0-6-0 (1926)												
64912	5F: J39 0-6-0 (1926)												
64930	5F: J39 0-6-0 (1926)												
64932	5F: J39 0-6-0 (1926)												
64948	5F: J39 0-6-0 (1926)												
64964	5F: J39 0-6-0 (1926)												
62732	4P: D49 4-4-0 (1927)												
62734	4P: D49 4-4-0 (1927)												
43139	4MT 2-6-0 (1947)		NEW	X	X	X	X	X	X	X	X	X	
69139	3F: N15 0-6-2T (1910)												
69155	3F: N15 0-6-2T (1910)												
69174	3F: N15 0-6-2T (1910)												
69185	3F: N15 0-6-2T (1910)	To Eastfield	X	X	X	X	X	X	X	X	X	X	X
69197	3F: N15 0-6-2T (1910)	To Eastfield	X	X	X	X	X	X	X	X	X	X	
69215	3F: N15 0-6-2T (1910)												
69218	3F: N15 0-6-2T (1910)	To Eastfield	X	X	X	X	X	X	X	X	X	X	X
64461	3F: J35 0-6-0 (1906)	X	X	X	Ex Stirling		To Parkhead	X	X	X	X	X	X
64471	3F: J35 0-6-0 (1906)	X	X	X	Ex Stirling								X
64478	3F: J35 0-6-0 (1906)												
64499	3F: J35 0-6-0 (1906)											X	
64511	3F: J35 0-6-0 (1906)											X	
64526	3F: J35 0-6-0 (1906)												
62281	2P: D31 4-4-0 (1890)												
67458	2P: C15 4-4-2T (1911)												
67474	2P: C15 4-4-2T (1911)												
67481	2P: C15 4-4-2T (1911)												
65216	2F: J36 0-6-0 (1888)												
65293	2F: J36 0-6-0 (1888)												
65304	2F: J36 0-6-0 (1888)												
65312	2F: J36 0-6-0 (1888)												
65321	2F: J36 0-6-0 (1888)												
12084	0F: Diesel 0-6-0												
12085	0F: Diesel 0-6-0												
12086	0F: Diesel 0-6-0												

Making a noise like a jazz-band, Haymarket V2 60814 stands in for an A3 Pacific and climbs through Fushiebridge on the way to Falahill with an Edinburgh - Carlisle semi-fast. The fireman has just placed a 'bit round the edges' and is watching the results via the chimney. (W.S.Sellar)

Engine	Class	Aug-52	Sep-52	Oct-52	Nov-52	Dec-52	Jan-53	Feb-53	Mar-53	Apr-53	May-53	Jun-53	Jul-53
	LOCOMOTIVE ALLOCATION & MOVEMENTS : CARLISLE (CANAL) - 12B												
60068	7P: A3 4-6-2 (1922)												
60079	7P: A3 4-6-2 (1922)												
60093	7P: A3 4-6-2 (1922)												
60095	7P: A3 4-6-2 (1922)												
60111	7P: A3 4-6-2 (1922)												
61851	6F: K3 2-6-0 (1924)												
61854	6F: K3 2-6-0 (1924)												
61858	6F: K3 2-6-0 (1924)												
61882	6F: K3 2-6-0 (1924)												
61898	6F: K3 2-6-0 (1924)												
61916	6F: K3 2-6-0 (1924)												
61936	6F: K3 2-6-0 (1924)												
61937	6F: K3 2-6-0 (1924)												
61217	5MT: B1 4-6-0 (1942)												
61219	5MT: B1 4-6-0 (1942)												
61222	5MT: B1 4-6-0 (1942)												
61395	5MT: B1 4-6-0 (1942)												
44790	5MT 4-6-0 (1934)												
44792	5MT 4-6-0 (1934)												
64727	5F: J39 0-6-0 (1926)												
64733	5F: J39 0-6-0 (1926)												
64875	5F: J39 0-6-0 (1926)												
64877	5F: J39 0-6-0 (1926)												
64880	5F: J39 0-6-0 (1926)												
64884	5F: J39 0-6-0 (1926)												
64888	5F: J39 0-6-0 (1926)												
64895	5F: J39 0-6-0 (1926)												
64899	5F: J39 0-6-0 (1926)												
64912	5F: J39 0-6-0 (1926)												
64930	5F: J39 0-6-0 (1926)												
64932	5F: J39 0-6-0 (1926)												
64948	5F: J39 0-6-0 (1926)												
64964	5F: J39 0-6-0 (1926)												
62732	4P: D49 4-4-0 (1927)												
62734	4P: D49 4-4-0 (1927)												
43139	4MT 2-6-0 (1947)												
69139	3F: N15 0-6-2T (1910)												
69155	3F: N15 0-6-2T (1910)												
69174	3F: N15 0-6-2T (1910)												
69215	3F: N15 0-6-2T (1910)												
64471	3F: J35 0-6-0 (1906)												
64478	3F: J35 0-6-0 (1906)												
64499	3F: J35 0-6-0 (1906)												
64511	3F: J35 0-6-0 (1906)												
64526	3F: J35 0-6-0 (1906)												
62281	2P: D31 4-4-0 (1890)					W/D	X	X	X	X	X	X	X
67458	2P: C15 4-4-2T (1911)												
67474	2P: C15 4-4-2T (1911)												
67481	2P: C15 4-4-2T (1911)												
65216	2F: J36 0-6-0 (1888)												
65293	2F: J36 0-6-0 (1888)												
65304	2F: J36 0-6-0 (1888)												
65312	2F: J36 0-6-0 (1888)												
65321	2F: J36 0-6-0 (1888)												
12084	0F: Diesel 0-6-0												
12085	0F: Diesel 0-6-0												
12086	0F: Diesel 0-6-0												

A B1 4-6-0 on a stopping train was not an especially unusual sight but the appearance of 61025 which was allocated to Tweedmouth was certainly worthy of note. The wanderer was noted working the 16.10 Edinburgh - Hawick through Fushiebridge on the 23 May 1959. 61025's usual duty was on the 07.13 Berwick to Edinburgh and the 17.55 Edinburgh to Berwick. Prior to 1939 the 16.10 used to include a two-coach portion for Berwick via St Boswells and Kelso. (W.S.Sellar)

Engine	Class	Aug-53	Sep-53	Oct-53	Nov-53	Dec-53	Jan-54	Feb-54	Mar-54	Apr-54	May-54	Jun-54	Jul-54
60037	7P: A3 4-6-2 (1922)	X	X	X	X	X	X	X	Ex Haymarket	To Haymarket	X	X	X
60068	7P: A3 4-6-2 (1922)												
60079	7P: A3 4-6-2 (1922)												
60093	7P: A3 4-6-2 (1922)												
60095	7P: A3 4-6-2 (1922)												
60097	7P: A3 4-6-2 (1922)	X	X	X	X	Ex Haymarket	To Haymarket	X	X	X	X	X	X
60111	7P: A3 4-6-2 (1922)												
61851	6F: K3 2-6-0 (1924)												
61854	6F: K3 2-6-0 (1924)												
61858	6F: K3 2-6-0 (1924)												
61882	6F: K3 2-6-0 (1924)												
61898	6F: K3 2-6-0 (1924)												
61916	6F: K3 2-6-0 (1924)												
61936	6F: K3 2-6-0 (1924)												
61937	6F: K3 2-6-0 (1924)												
61217	5MT: B1 4-6-0 (1942)												
61219	5MT: B1 4-6-0 (1942)												
61222	5MT: B1 4-6-0 (1942)												
61239	5MT: B1 4-6-0 (1942)	X	X	Ex York									
61290	5MT: B1 4-6-0 (1942)	X	X	Ex Stockton									
61395	5MT: B1 4-6-0 (1942)												
44790	5MT 4-6-0 (1934)		To Kingmoor	X	X	X	X	X	X	X	X	X	X
44792	5MT 4-6-0 (1934)		To Kingmoor	X	X	X	X	X	X	X	X	X	X
64727	5F: J39 0-6-0 (1926)												
64733	5F: J39 0-6-0 (1926)												
64875	5F: J39 0-6-0 (1926)												
64877	5F: J39 0-6-0 (1926)												
64880	5F: J39 0-6-0 (1926)												
64884	5F: J39 0-6-0 (1926)												
64888	5F: J39 0-6-0 (1926)												
64895	5F: J39 0-6-0 (1926)												
64899	5F: J39 0-6-0 (1926)												
64912	5F: J39 0-6-0 (1926)												
64930	5F: J39 0-6-0 (1926)												
64932	5F: J39 0-6-0 (1926)												
64948	5F: J39 0-6-0 (1926)												
64964	5F: J39 0-6-0 (1926)												
62732	4P: D49 4-4-0 (1927)												
62734	4P: D49 4-4-0 (1927)												
43139	4MT 2-6-0 (1947)												
69139	3F: N15 0-6-2T (1910)												
69155	3F: N15 0-6-2T (1910)												
69174	3F: N15 0-6-2T (1910)												
69215	3F: N15 0-6-2T (1910)												
64471	3F: J35 0-6-0 (1906)												
64478	3F: J35 0-6-0 (1906)												
64499	3F: J35 0-6-0 (1906)												
64511	3F: J35 0-6-0 (1906)												
64526	3F: J35 0-6-0 (1906)												
67458	2P: C15 4-4-2T (1911)												
67474	2P: C15 4-4-2T (1911)												
67481	2P: C15 4-4-2T (1911)												
65216	2F: J36 0-6-0 (1888)												
65293	2F: J36 0-6-0 (1888)												
65304	2F: J36 0-6-0 (1888)												
65312	2F: J36 0-6-0 (1888)												
65321	2F: J36 0-6-0 (1888)												
12084	0F: Diesel 0-6-0												
12085	0F: Diesel 0-6-0												
12086	0F: Diesel 0-6-0												

LOCOMOTIVE ALLOCATION & MOVEMENTS : CARLISLE (CANAL) - 12B

K3 61858 of Carlisle (Canal) climbs the 1 in 70 bank through Fushiebridge in May 1959 with an Edinburgh (Niddrie) to Carlisle express goods. The crew will work as far as Hawick where they will exchange footplates with a down train and return to Edinburgh. The relaxed attitude of the fireman has less to do with the appetite of 61858 than with the exertions of the banker, J36 0-6-0 65224 (right) of St Margarets, which seems to be doing more than its share of work. (W.S.Sellar)

Engine	Class	Aug-54	Sep-54	Oct-54	Nov-54	Dec-54	Jan-55	Feb-55	Mar-55	Apr-55	May-55	Jun-55	Jul-55
	LOCOMOTIVE ALLOCATION & MOVEMENTS : CARLISLE (CANAL) - 12B												
60068	7P: A3 4-6-2 (1922)												
60079	7P: A3 4-6-2 (1922)												
60093	7P: A3 4-6-2 (1922)												
60095	7P: A3 4-6-2 (1922)												
60111	7P: A3 4-6-2 (1922)										To Leicester	X	X	X
61851	6F: K3 2-6-0 (1924)												
61854	6F: K3 2-6-0 (1924)												
61858	6F: K3 2-6-0 (1924)												
61882	6F: K3 2-6-0 (1924)												
61898	6F: K3 2-6-0 (1924)												
61916	6F: K3 2-6-0 (1924)												
61936	6F: K3 2-6-0 (1924)												
61937	6F: K3 2-6-0 (1924)												
61064	5MT: B1 4-6-0 (1942)	X	X	X	X	X	X	X	X	X	Ex Eastfield		
61217	5MT: B1 4-6-0 (1942)												
61219	5MT: B1 4-6-0 (1942)												
61222	5MT: B1 4-6-0 (1942)												
61239	5MT: B1 4-6-0 (1942)												
61290	5MT: B1 4-6-0 (1942)												
61395	5MT: B1 4-6-0 (1942)												
64727	5F: J39 0-6-0 (1926)												
64733	5F: J39 0-6-0 (1926)												
64875	5F: J39 0-6-0 (1926)												
64877	5F: J39 0-6-0 (1926)												
64880	5F: J39 0-6-0 (1926)												
64884	5F: J39 0-6-0 (1926)												
64888	5F: J39 0-6-0 (1926)												
64895	5F: J39 0-6-0 (1926)												
64899	5F: J39 0-6-0 (1926)												
64912	5F: J39 0-6-0 (1926)												
64930	5F: J39 0-6-0 (1926)												
64932	5F: J39 0-6-0 (1926)												
64948	5F: J39 0-6-0 (1926)												
64964	5F: J39 0-6-0 (1926)												
62732	4P: D49 4-4-0 (1927)												
62734	4P: D49 4-4-0 (1927)												
43139	4MT 2-6-0 (1947)												
69139	3F: N15 0-6-2T (1910)												
69155	3F: N15 0-6-2T (1910)												
69174	3F: N15 0-6-2T (1910)												
69215	3F: N15 0-6-2T (1910)												
64471	3F: J35 0-6-0 (1906)			To Polmadie	X	X	X	X	X	X	X	X	X
64478	3F: J35 0-6-0 (1906)												
64499	3F: J35 0-6-0 (1906)												
64511	3F: J35 0-6-0 (1906)						To Polmadie	X	X	X	X	X	X
64526	3F: J35 0-6-0 (1906)												
67458	2P: C15 4-4-2T (1911)												
67474	2P: C15 4-4-2T (1911)	To Eastfield	X	X	X	X	X	X	X	X	X	X	X
67481	2P: C15 4-4-2T (1911)												
65216	2F: J36 0-6-0 (1888)												
65293	2F: J36 0-6-0 (1888)												
65304	2F: J36 0-6-0 (1888)												
65312	2F: J36 0-6-0 (1888)												
65321	2F: J36 0-6-0 (1888)												
12084	0F: Diesel 0-6-0												
12085	0F: Diesel 0-6-0												
12086	0F: Diesel 0-6-0												

J36 0-6-0 65224 brings up the rear of the Carlisle-bound train (left) and there seems no doubt that the fireman is having to work for his money. 65224 was one of four bankers based at Hardengreen, the duties of which were to assist goods trains up the ten mile bank to Falahill. Each cycle of banking took about seventy minutes to complete. (W.S.Sellar)

Engine	Class	Aug-55	Sep-55	Oct-55	Nov-55	Dec-55	Jan-56	Feb-56	Mar-56	Apr-56	May-56	Jun-56	Jul-56
60068	7P: A3 4-6-2 (1922)												
60079	7P: A3 4-6-2 (1922)												
60093	7P: A3 4-6-2 (1922)												
60095	7P: A3 4-6-2 (1922)												
61851	6F: K3 2-6-0 (1924)												
61854	6F: K3 2-6-0 (1924)												
61858	6F: K3 2-6-0 (1924)												
61882	6F: K3 2-6-0 (1924)												
61898	6F: K3 2-6-0 (1924)												
61916	6F: K3 2-6-0 (1924)												
61936	6F: K3 2-6-0 (1924)												
61937	6F: K3 2-6-0 (1924)												
61064	5MT: B1 4-6-0 (1942)												
61217	5MT: B1 4-6-0 (1942)												
61219	5MT: B1 4-6-0 (1942)												
61222	5MT: B1 4-6-0 (1942)												
61239	5MT: B1 4-6-0 (1942)												
61290	5MT: B1 4-6-0 (1942)												
61395	5MT: B1 4-6-0 (1942)												
64727	5F: J39 0-6-0 (1926)												
64733	5F: J39 0-6-0 (1926)												
64875	5F: J39 0-6-0 (1926)												
64877	5F: J39 0-6-0 (1926)												
64880	5F: J39 0-6-0 (1926)												
64884	5F: J39 0-6-0 (1926)												
64888	5F: J39 0-6-0 (1926)												
64895	5F: J39 0-6-0 (1926)												
64899	5F: J39 0-6-0 (1926)												
64912	5F: J39 0-6-0 (1926)												
64930	5F: J39 0-6-0 (1926)												
64932	5F: J39 0-6-0 (1926)												
64948	5F: J39 0-6-0 (1926)												
64964	5F: J39 0-6-0 (1926)												
62732	4P: D49 4-4-0 (1927)												
62734	4P: D49 4-4-0 (1927)												
43139	4MT 2-6-0 (1947)												
69139	3F: N15 0-6-2T (1910)												
69155	3F: N15 0-6-2T (1910)												
69174	3F: N15 0-6-2T (1910)												
69215	3F: N15 0-6-2T (1910)												
64478	3F: J35 0-6-0 (1906)												
64499	3F: J35 0-6-0 (1906)												
64526	3F: J35 0-6-0 (1906)												
67458	2P: C15 4-4-2T (1911)												
67481	2P: C15 4-4-2T (1911)						W/D	X	X	X	X	X	X
65216	2F: J36 0-6-0 (1888)												
65293	2F: J36 0-6-0 (1888)												
65304	2F: J36 0-6-0 (1888)												
65312	2F: J36 0-6-0 (1888)												
65321	2F: J36 0-6-0 (1888)												
12084	0F: Diesel 0-6-0												
12085	0F: Diesel 0-6-0												
12086	0F: Diesel 0-6-0												

Knowing that Britannia Pacific 70038 'Robin Hood' had been allocated to the 10.40 Edinburgh - Pontypridd special with 70037 'Hereward the Wake' booked to a following excursion on 7 February 1965, the photographer positioned himself on the 1 in 70 between Borthwick Bank and Tynehead in the expectation of a couple of good pictures. He got more than he bargained for since 70038 failed in the vicinity of Gorebridge and 70037 was used to assist the failure to Falahill. (W.S.Sellar)

Engine	Class	Aug-56	Sep-56	Oct-56	Nov-56	Dec-56	Jan-57	Feb-57	Mar-57	Apr-57	May-57	Jun-57	Jul-57
	LOCOMOTIVE ALLOCATION & MOVEMENTS : CARLISLE (CANAL) - 12B												
60068	7P: A3 4-6-2 (1922)												
60079	7P: A3 4-6-2 (1922)												
60093	7P: A3 4-6-2 (1922)												
60095	7P: A3 4-6-2 (1922)												
61851	6F: K3 2-6-0 (1924)												
61854	6F: K3 2-6-0 (1924)								To Hull (D)	X	X	X	X
61858	6F: K3 2-6-0 (1924)												
61882	6F: K3 2-6-0 (1924)												
61898	6F: K3 2-6-0 (1924)												
61916	6F: K3 2-6-0 (1924)												
61936	6F: K3 2-6-0 (1924)												
61937	6F: K3 2-6-0 (1924)												
61064	5MT: B1 4-6-0 (1942)												
61217	5MT: B1 4-6-0 (1942)												
61219	5MT: B1 4-6-0 (1942)												
61222	5MT: B1 4-6-0 (1942)												
61239	5MT: B1 4-6-0 (1942)												
61290	5MT: B1 4-6-0 (1942)												
61395	5MT: B1 4-6-0 (1942)												
64727	5F: J39 0-6-0 (1926)												
64733	5F: J39 0-6-0 (1926)												
64875	5F: J39 0-6-0 (1926)												
64877	5F: J39 0-6-0 (1926)												
64880	5F: J39 0-6-0 (1926)												
64884	5F: J39 0-6-0 (1926)												
64888	5F: J39 0-6-0 (1926)												
64895	5F: J39 0-6-0 (1926)												
64899	5F: J39 0-6-0 (1926)												
64912	5F: J39 0-6-0 (1926)												
64930	5F: J39 0-6-0 (1926)												
64932	5F: J39 0-6-0 (1926)												
64948	5F: J39 0-6-0 (1926)												
64964	5F: J39 0-6-0 (1926)												
62732	4P: D49 4-4-0 (1927)												
62734	4P: D49 4-4-0 (1927)												
43139	4MT 2-6-0 (1947)												
69139	3F: N15 0-6-2T (1910)												
69155	3F: N15 0-6-2T (1910)												
69174	3F: N15 0-6-2T (1910)												
69215	3F: N15 0-6-2T (1910)												
64478	3F: J35 0-6-0 (1906)												
64499	3F: J35 0-6-0 (1906)												
64526	3F: J35 0-6-0 (1906)												
67458	2P: C15 4-4-2T (1911)						W/D	X	X	X	X	X	X
65216	2F: J36 0-6-0 (1888)					To Polmadie	X	X	X	X	X	X	X
65293	2F: J36 0-6-0 (1888)												
65304	2F: J36 0-6-0 (1888)					To Polmadie	X	X	X	X	X	X	X
65312	2F: J36 0-6-0 (1888)												
65321	2F: J36 0-6-0 (1888)												
12084	0F: Diesel 0-6-0												
12085	0F: Diesel 0-6-0												
12086	0F: Diesel 0-6-0												

Evidently not in the prime of condition itself, 70037 'Hereward the Wake' assists 70038 'Robin Hood' and its ten coach load up the 1 in 70 near Tynehead. (W.S.Sellar)

Engine	Class	Aug-57	Sep-57	Oct-57	Nov-57	Dec-57	Jan-58	Feb-58	Mar-58	Apr-58	May-58	Jun-58	Jul-58
	LOCOMOTIVE ALLOCATION & MOVEMENTS : CARLISLE (CANAL) - 12B												
60068	7P: A3 4-6-2 (1922)												
60079	7P: A3 4-6-2 (1922)												
60093	7P: A3 4-6-2 (1922)												
60095	7P: A3 4-6-2 (1922)												
61851	6F: K3 2-6-0 (1924)												
61858	6F: K3 2-6-0 (1924)												
61882	6F: K3 2-6-0 (1924)												
61898	6F: K3 2-6-0 (1924)												
61916	6F: K3 2-6-0 (1924)												
61936	6F: K3 2-6-0 (1924)												
61937	6F: K3 2-6-0 (1924)												
61064	5MT: B1 4-6-0 (1942)												
61217	5MT: B1 4-6-0 (1942)												
61219	5MT: B1 4-6-0 (1942)					To E'bro (H)	X	X	X	X	X	X	X
61222	5MT: B1 4-6-0 (1942)												
61239	5MT: B1 4-6-0 (1942)												
61290	5MT: B1 4-6-0 (1942)												
61395	5MT: B1 4-6-0 (1942)												
64727	5F: J39 0-6-0 (1926)												
64733	5F: J39 0-6-0 (1926)												
64875	5F: J39 0-6-0 (1926)												
64877	5F: J39 0-6-0 (1926)												
64880	5F: J39 0-6-0 (1926)												
64884	5F: J39 0-6-0 (1926)												
64888	5F: J39 0-6-0 (1926)												
64895	5F: J39 0-6-0 (1926)												
64899	5F: J39 0-6-0 (1926)												
64912	5F: J39 0-6-0 (1926)												
64930	5F: J39 0-6-0 (1926)												
64932	5F: J39 0-6-0 (1926)												
64948	5F: J39 0-6-0 (1926)												
64964	5F: J39 0-6-0 (1926)												
62732	4P: D49 4-4-0 (1927)												
62734	4P: D49 4-4-0 (1927)												
43139	4MT 2-6-0 (1947)												
44157	4F 0-6-0 (1924)	X	X	X	X	X	X	X	X	X	X	X	Ex Nuneaton
44292	4F 0-6-0 (1924)	X	X	X	X	X	X	X	X	X	X	X	Ex Nuneaton
69564	3P: N2 0-6-2T (1925)	X	Ex Parkhead										
69139	3F: N15 0-6-2T (1910)									W/D	X	X	X
69155	3F: N15 0-6-2T (1910)												
69174	3F: N15 0-6-2T (1910)												
69215	3F: N15 0-6-2T (1910)												
64478	3F: J35 0-6-0 (1906)												
64499	3F: J35 0-6-0 (1906)												
64526	3F: J35 0-6-0 (1906)								W/D	X	X	X	X
47662	3F 0-6-0T (1924)	X	X	X	X	X	X	X	X	Ex Crewe (S)			
46433	2MT 2-6-0 (1946)	X	X	X	X	X	X	X	X	X	X	Ex Rhyl	
65293	2F: J36 0-6-0 (1888)												
65312	2F: J36 0-6-0 (1888)												
65321	2F: J36 0-6-0 (1888)												
12084	0F: Diesel 0-6-0												
12085	0F: Diesel 0-6-0												
12086	0F: Diesel 0-6-0												

The improvements made to the A3 Pacifics by the Kylchap blastpipe and German deflectors cannot be understated and raised the class from class 7 to class 8 even though the improvement was never formally recognised. 60062 'Prince Palatine, passes Borthwick Bank with a troop special on 19th June 1965. (W.S.Sellar)

Engine	Class	Aug-58	Sep-58	Oct-58	Nov-58	Dec-58	Jan-59	Feb-59	Mar-59	Apr-59	May-59	Jun-59	Jul-59
LOCOMOTIVE ALLOCATION & MOVEMENTS : CARLISLE (CANAL) - 12B													
60068	7P: A3 4-6-2 (1922)												
60079	7P: A3 4-6-2 (1922)												
60093	7P: A3 4-6-2 (1922)												
60095	7P: A3 4-6-2 (1922)												
61851	6F: K3 2-6-0 (1924)											To March	X
61858	6F: K3 2-6-0 (1924)												
61882	6F: K3 2-6-0 (1924)									To W. Halse	X	X	X
61898	6F: K3 2-6-0 (1924)							W/D	X	X	X	X	X
61916	6F: K3 2-6-0 (1924)												
61936	6F: K3 2-6-0 (1924)												
61937	6F: K3 2-6-0 (1924)											To March	X
61064	5MT: B1 4-6-0 (1942)												
61217	5MT: B1 4-6-0 (1942)												
61222	5MT: B1 4-6-0 (1942)												
61239	5MT: B1 4-6-0 (1942)												
61290	5MT: B1 4-6-0 (1942)												
61395	5MT: B1 4-6-0 (1942)												
64727	5F: J39 0-6-0 (1926)				To Gorton	X	X	X	X	X	X	X	X
64733	5F: J39 0-6-0 (1926)												
64875	5F: J39 0-6-0 (1926)				To Gorton	X	X	X	X	X	X	X	X
64877	5F: J39 0-6-0 (1926)												
64880	5F: J39 0-6-0 (1926)												
64884	5F: J39 0-6-0 (1926)												
64888	5F: J39 0-6-0 (1926)												
64895	5F: J39 0-6-0 (1926)												
64899	5F: J39 0-6-0 (1926)												
64912	5F: J39 0-6-0 (1926)												
64930	5F: J39 0-6-0 (1926)				To Gorton	X	X	X	X	X	X	X	X
64932	5F: J39 0-6-0 (1926)												
64948	5F: J39 0-6-0 (1926)												
64964	5F: J39 0-6-0 (1926)												
62732	4P: D49 4-4-0 (1927)			To Darlington	X	X	X	X	X	X	X	X	X
62734	4P: D49 4-4-0 (1927)												
62747	4P: D49 4-4-0 (1927)	X	X	X	Ex York								
43139	4MT 2-6-0 (1947)												
44157	4F 0-6-0 (1924)												
44292	4F 0-6-0 (1924)	To Work'ton	X	X	X	X	X	X	X	X	X	X	X
69564	3P: N2 0-6-2T (1925)												
69155	3F: N15 0-6-2T (1910)												
69174	3F: N15 0-6-2T (1910)				W/D	X	X	X	X	X	X	X	X
69215	3F: N15 0-6-2T (1910)												
64478	3F: J35 0-6-0 (1906)												
64499	3F: J35 0-6-0 (1906)												
47662	3F 0-6-0T (1924)	To Work'ton	X	X	X	X	X	X	X	X	X	X	X
46433	2MT 2-6-0 (1946)	To Work'ton	X	X	X	X	X	X	X	X	X	X	X
65237	2F: J36 0-6-0 (1888)	X	X	X	X	X	Ex Eastfield						
65293	2F: J36 0-6-0 (1888)												
65312	2F: J36 0-6-0 (1888)												
65321	2F: J36 0-6-0 (1888)												
12084	0F: Diesel 0-6-0												
12085	0F: Diesel 0-6-0												
12086	0F: Diesel 0-6-0												

1962 was the year in which the familiar K3 2-6-0's were swept away leaving services to the mercies of a rather unreliable fleet of diesels. On 19th June 1965 matters reached such a low ebb that B1 4-6-0 61029 'Chamois' had to be turned out for the 13.35 Millerhill - Carlisle goods and is seen passing Falahill summit. 61029 was far from being the only B1 to come to the rescue of diesels in those days. (W.S.Sellar)

Engine	Class	Aug-59	Sep-59	Oct-59	Nov-59	Dec-59	Jan-60	Feb-60	Mar-60	Apr-60	May-60	Jun-60	Jul-60
	LOCOMOTIVE ALLOCATION & MOVEMENTS : CARLISLE (CANAL) - 12C												
60068	7P: A3 4-6-2 (1922)												
60079	7P: A3 4-6-2 (1922)												
60093	7P: A3 4-6-2 (1922)												
60095	7P: A3 4-6-2 (1922)												
61851	6F: K3 2-6-0 (1924)	X	X	X	X	X	X	X	Ex March			To W. Halse	X
61858	6F: K3 2-6-0 (1924)												
61916	6F: K3 2-6-0 (1924)												
61936	6F: K3 2-6-0 (1924)												
61937	6F: K3 2-6-0 (1924)	X	X	X	X	X	X	Ex March	W/D	X	X	X	X
61064	5MT: B1 4-6-0 (1942)												
61217	5MT: B1 4-6-0 (1942)												
61222	5MT: B1 4-6-0 (1942)												
61239	5MT: B1 4-6-0 (1942)												
61290	5MT: B1 4-6-0 (1942)												
61395	5MT: B1 4-6-0 (1942)												
64733	5F: J39 0-6-0 (1926)												
64877	5F: J39 0-6-0 (1926)												
64880	5F: J39 0-6-0 (1926)												
64884	5F: J39 0-6-0 (1926)												
64888	5F: J39 0-6-0 (1926)												
64895	5F: J39 0-6-0 (1926)												
64899	5F: J39 0-6-0 (1926)												
64912	5F: J39 0-6-0 (1926)				W/D	X	X	X	X	X	X	X	X
64932	5F: J39 0-6-0 (1926)												
64948	5F: J39 0-6-0 (1926)					W/D	X	X	X	X	X	X	X
64964	5F: J39 0-6-0 (1926)												
62734	4P: D49 4-4-0 (1927)												
62747	4P: D49 4-4-0 (1927)												
43139	4MT 2-6-0 (1947)												
44157	4F 0-6-0 (1924)												
69564	3P: N2 0-6-2T (1925)												
69155	3F: N15 0-6-2T (1910)												
69215	3F: N15 0-6-2T (1910)				W/D	X	X	X	X	X	X	X	X
64478	3F: J35 0-6-0 (1906)												
64499	3F: J35 0-6-0 (1906)												
65237	2F: J36 0-6-0 (1888)												
65293	2F: J36 0-6-0 (1888)												
65312	2F: J36 0-6-0 (1888)												
65321	2F: J36 0-6-0 (1888)												
12084	0F: Diesel 0-6-0												
12085	0F: Diesel 0-6-0												
12086	0F: Diesel 0-6-0												
13171	0F: Diesel 0-6-0	X	X	X	Ex Upperby								

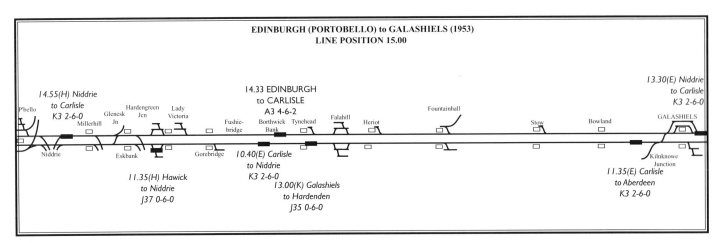

EDINBURGH (PORTOBELLO) to GALASHIELS (1953)
LINE POSITION 15.00

14.55(H) Niddrie to Carlisle K3 2-6-0

14.33 EDINBURGH to CARLISLE A3 4-6-2

13.30(E) Niddrie to Carlisle K3 2-6-0

P'bello — Niddrie — Millerhill — Eskbank — Hardengreen Jcn — Glenesk Jn — Lady Victoria — Gorebridge — Fushiebridge — Borthwick Bank — Tynehead — Falahill — Heriot — Fountainhall — Stow — Bowland — GALASHIELS — Kilnknowe Junction

11.35(H) Hawick to Niddrie J37 0-6-0

10.40(E) Carlisle to Niddrie K3 2-6-0

13.00(K) Galashiels to Hardenden J35 0-6-0

11.35(E) Carlisle to Aberdeen K3 2-6-0

CONTROLLER'S LOG: While the V1/V3 2-6-2T's are irregular visitors to the Waverley route and almost unknown south of Galashiels, their C15 4-4-2 predecessors continue to do work on the line and five of the class ruminate at Hawick - the verb being chosen advisedly since the availability of the class can fall to the unspeakably low - and include in their duties the cross-country branch service between St Boswells and Berwick on Tweed.

The thirty-five mile route, which runs sheds with a C15 from the former and a G5 from the latter covering the passenger services. A St Boswells' J36 0-6-0 looks after the goods workings to Kelso and Jedburgh while through goods traffic is catered for by a North Eastern J39 0-6-0 which works the 13.50 Tweedmouth - St Boswells and the 16.55 return.

Since the line is passed for the heaviest of engines, some surprising visitors can appear when the booked engines are unavailable and it is by no means unknown for a K3 2-6-0 to trip to Kelso which has just arrived back in time to connect into the 13.26 Carlisle - Edinburgh.

With two trains approaching from both directions, the line around Whitrope summit is probably an interesting place to be. The up train is an Aberdeen - Carlisle goods with a K3 2-6-0 on the front and a J36 0-6-0 banker in the rear. The down train, the 13.35 Canal to Niddrie, is a single-engine load because the pilot has to remain at Newcastleton for the heavier 14.35 Carlisle - Meadows which is

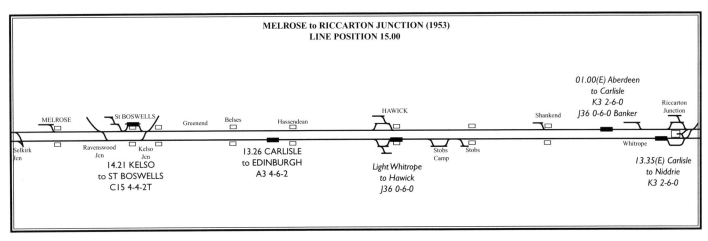

MELROSE to RICCARTON JUNCTION (1953)
LINE POSITION 15.00

01.00(E) Aberdeen to Carlisle K3 2-6-0 J36 0-6-0 Banker

MELROSE — St BOSWELLS — Greenend — Belses — Hassendean — HAWICK — Stobs Camp — Stobs — Shankend — Whitrope — Riccarton Junction

Selkirk Jcn — Ravenswood Jcn — Kelso Jcn

14.21 KELSO to ST BOSWELLS C15 4-4-2T

13.26 CARLISLE to EDINBURGH A3 4-6-2

Light Whitrope to Hawick J36 0-6-0

13.35(E) Carlisle to Niddrie K3 2-6-0

through some of the most sparsely populated areas imaginable and occasionally makes the headlines when it is used for East Coast diversions - it is maintained to accept RA9 locomotives in an emergency - has quite a respectable service of trains worked by a varied assortment of locomotives which include a C15 4-4-2T, a J36 0-6-0, a G5 0-4-4T and a J39 0-6-0. In addition Sentinel 68138 is shedded at Kelso and shunts the yard there from 09.00 to 17.00.

Making an end-on connection with the North Eastern at Sprouston, the duties on the line are divided between St Boswells and Tweedmouth appear on the two-coach passenger trains.

Until August 1948 when it was severed by floods, the Ravenswood Junction - Reston branch gave a second through route between St Boswells and Berwick with four through passenger trains a day in each direction. When the line was severed, the passenger service was withdrawn leaving only a daily goods service (06.10 ex St Boswells) to and from Greenlaw.

The train that can be seen standing in St Boswells is the North British contribution to the line - the North Eastern usually provide a G5 0-4-4T - whose C15 tank works the morning and evening services to Berwick plus the afternoon passing Riddings Junction. The question of single and double engine loads is one on which decisions are taken whilst the train is being made up in Canal Yard and if traffic is heavy, the planned arrangements will be over-ridden; the bankers being organised on an impromptu basis. (For example the banker waiting for the 14.35 ex Carlisle can be used for the 13.35 while the J36 that has assisted the 01.00 ex Aberdeen to Whitrope can run light behind the Aberdeen train to Newcastleton to bank the 14.35).

The Pacific that worked the 21.05 St Pancras earlier this morning can be seen approaching Tynehead with the 14.33 stopping train.

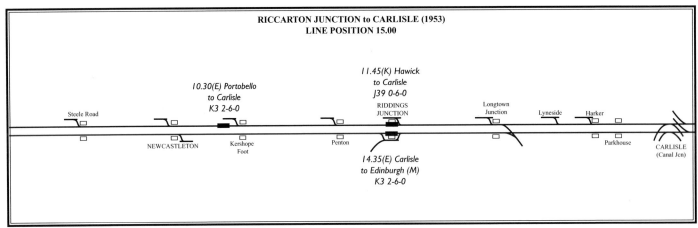

RICCARTON JUNCTION to CARLISLE (1953)
LINE POSITION 15.00

10.30(E) Portobello to Carlisle K3 2-6-0

11.45(K) Hawick to Carlisle J39 0-6-0

Steele Road — NEWCASTLETON — Kershope Foot — Penton — RIDDINGS JUNCTION — Longtown Junction — Lyneside — Harker — Parkhouse — CARLISLE (Canal Jcn)

14.35(E) Carlisle to Edinburgh (M) K3 2-6-0

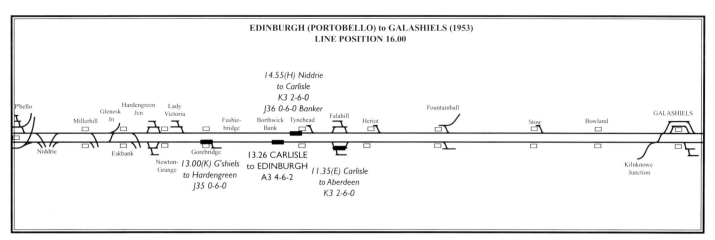

EDINBURGH (PORTOBELLO) to GALASHIELS (1953)
LINE POSITION 16.00

CONTROLLER'S LOG : " - Gorebridge. The trip's ready. Shall I let it out now?"

The signalman is referring to the 13.00 Galashiels to Hardengreen which has completed its work and is ready to leave. Under normal circumstances it would be held until the 13.26 express from Carlisle - now passing Fushiebridge - had passed but the circumstances are not normal because when the trip terminates at Hardengreen, the crew have just enough time to work a train to Niddrie or Portobello and back. If however they are delayed on the way in to Hardengreen - and a couple of minutes

then split it, the first twenty can be placed in the down refuge for the pilot then the engine can back onto the rest and right away Portobello up yard, main line. You'll need to tell the crew. They don't know they're going to Portobello."

Sometimes the driver or guard will come on the phone with a dozen assorted and mathematically pure reasons why they cannot possibly get to Portobello and back within their time and it pays to be ready for a blazing row. On this occasion however, they split the train and set off for Portobello without a murmur.

Gorebridge reports the express standing

D30 4-4-0 prepares to leave the sidings with the stock of a Newcastle train. Another D30 sits in the down platform waiting to depart with the 16.15 school train to St Boswells. The up main has been cleared for the Pacific-hauled 14.33 Edinburgh - Carlisle which runs as an express as far as Hawick before calling at most stations beyond. One envies the school children who live between Hawick and Riccarton Junction with their choice of an A3 or a D30.

One also envies those who reside on the Kelso line with their 4-4-2T - always assuming a member of the class is in a condition to fill the

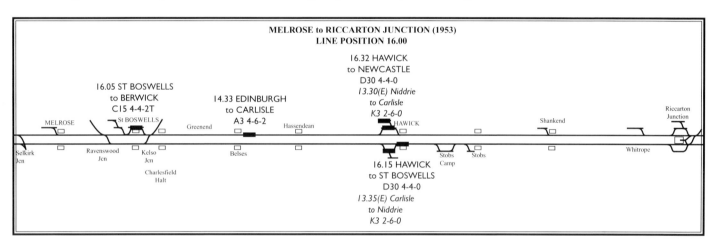

MELROSE to RICCARTON JUNCTION (1953)
LINE POSITION 16.00

can make the difference - they will be justified in refusing to take any further work since they would not be able to get back to Hardengreen without incurring overtime.

" - Let it go."

The express might be knocked for a minute or two but it is the lesser of two evils.

" - Hardengreen Junction? Next down is the Galashiels trip. Engine 64586 with thirty on. The ten on the brake are East Coasts via Portobello. When it arrives put it straight in the down loop - the express is right behind -

for two minutes "569 goods given preference Gorebridge to Hardengreen" is scrawled onto the traincard for the 13.26: a comment that will provoke a string of correspondence from the trains' clerk in a day or two's time. Droit de Controller, he will be told.

The 11.35 Carlisle to Aberdeen goods pulls out of the refuge at Falahill, having been shunted for the 13.26.

In the meantime there is an interesting jumble of trains collecting in the Hawick area. A pair of goods trains are exchanging crews as a

diagram - on the 16.05 St Boswells to Berwick.

In contrast to the D30's and C15's at Hawick and St Boswells, the English end of the line has more modern look to it as 4MT 2-6-0 43139 heads south with the 15.30 Langholm - Carlisle passenger and passes a St Margarets' B1 4-6-0 with the 15.37 Carlisle to Edinburgh stopping train. It can be seen that 43139 and its train are uncomfortably close to the Hawick - Carlisle trip which is on a tight margin and backing into Lyneside sidings. Doubtless another letter from the trains' clerk will be the result........

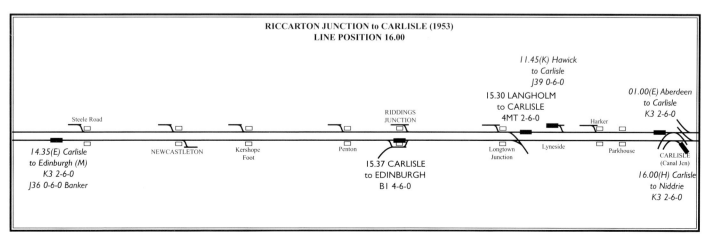

RICCARTON JUNCTION to CARLISLE (1953)
LINE POSITION 16.00

What little population the Waverley route served was contained within a narrow twenty-mile band that stretched from Galashiels to Hawick: too long to be served by a single centrally located station yet too important to be ignored.

The result was that after an hour's energetic running from Edinburgh, trains were required to stop no less than four times - Galashiels, Melrose, St Boswells and Hawick - before being able to regain the reigns of express running.

To foreign eyes used to the commercial rigours that governed the ordering of matters in the home counties, it seemed extraordinary that the daily London - Edinburgh express should ignore Bedford with its population of sixty thousand yet call at tiny Melrose which had a job to muster one-thirtieth of that figure.

Of these isthmus stations, St Boswells had a claim to being the most interesting on the grounds that it was - or at least, had been - the junction for two points on the East Coast main line: via Duns to Reston and via Kelso to Tweedmouth and Berwick.

Neither branch had flourished in postwar times and in fact the Reston line was in a terminally sorry state, having been severed between Duns and Greenlaw by the floods of 1948. Until that time the branch had been the recognised route for traffic between St Boswells and Berwick whilst the line via Tweedmouth - which survived until 1964 - had tended to focus upon Kelso.

From 1948 through running was switched to the Kelso route, which involved a reversal at Tweedmouth, leaving nothing on the Reston line except a morning goods trip from St Boswells to Greenlaw and a similar goods working from Tweedmouth to Duns. The gap made by the floods was never repaired.

During the rather austere early BR days both the Reston and Tweedmouth lines slipped somewhat into the background, the former all but disappearing in a spell of bad weather whilst the other regressed into quiet isolation, worked by a pair of carriage sets that each performed two round trips between Berwick and St Boswells.

This contrasted strongly with pre-war affairs when no less than six two-coach sets were needed to maintain the services on both branches. One of the differences between the two periods was that the primary route for Berwick services had been via Duns and Reston whilst on the Tweedmouth route, Kelso had been regarded as a terminus where one changed for the NER service to Berwick. Of the four services in 1938 that ran from St Boswells to Berwick, only one ran via Kelso.

TRAFFIC WORKING : ST BOSWELLS JUNCTION (1953)

Train	Arr	Engine	Dep	Destination
23.15 Falahill	00.09	J37 0-6-0	00.20	Hawick
22.00 Carlisle Canal	01.49	K3 2-6-0	(02.20)	Clover with 22.05 Dundee
22.05 Dundee West	02.09	A3 4-6-2	(02.25)	Clover with 22.00 Carlisle
(22.00 Carlisle Canal)	(01.49)	K3 2-6-0	02.20	Portobello
(22.05 ex Dundee)	(02.06)	A3 4-6-2	02.25	Carlisle Canal
23.10 Carlisle Canal	02.28	J35 0-6-0		
01.10 Carlisle Canal		A3 4-6-2	03.06	Dundee
20.20 Aberdeen		K3 2-6-0	03.08	Carlisle Canal
01.30 Carlisle Canal		V2 2-6-2	03.26	Perth (North)
00.55 Inverkeithing		K3 2-6-0	03.42	Carlisle Canal
01.00 Niddrie	04.02	J35 0-6-0		
00.10 Carlisle Canal		A3 4-6-2	04/17	Niddrie
		J36 0-6-0	04/50	Galashiels
02.25 Portobello	04.51	D49 4-4-0	05.01	Hawick
02.15 Carlisle Canal		V2 2-6-2	05/09	Edinburgh (Meadows)
04.10 EDINBURGH	05.26	B1 4-6-0	05.31	HAWICK
05.15 Galashiels (EBV)	05.35	J36 0-6-0		
04.08 CARLISLE	05.45	A4 4-6-2	05.50	EDINBURGH
		J36 0-6-0	06.10	Greenlaw
22.25 Aberdeen		K3 2-6-0	06/14	Carlisle Canal
		C15: SB2	06.22	BERWICK
		J35 0-6-0	06.45	Kelso
21.05 ST PANCRAS	06.43	A3 4-6-2	06.47	EDINBURGH
06.49 HAWICK	07.06	D49 4-4-0	07.08	EDINBURGH
05.05 Portobello	07.08	J37 0-6-0	07.18	Hawick
23.05 Dundee		A3 4-6-2	07/37	Carlisle Canal
04.20 Carlisle Canal		K3 2-6-0	07/52	Portobello
06.30 BERWICK	08.07	G5 0-4-4T		
06.35 EDINBURGH	08.09	B1 4-6-0	08.13	CARLISLE
08.07 HAWICK	08.28	B1 4-6-0	08.30	EDINBURGH
		G5 0-4-4T	08.33	BERWICK
06.05 Carlisle Canal		B1 4-6-0	09/09	Aberdeen
00.30 Dundee West		K3 2-6-0	09/10	Carlisle Canal
09.00 Hawick	09.29	J37 0-6-0	09.40	Portobello
08.10 Greenlaw	09.50	J36 0-6-0		
08.35 EDINBURGH	10.02	B1 4-6-0	10.04	HAWICK
08.00 Carlisle Canal		K3 2-6-0	10/38	Perth
09.20 BERWICK	10.56	C15 4-4-2T		
09.05 CARLISLE	11.09	A3 4-6-2	11.13	EDINBURGH
10.05 EDINBURGH	11.14	A3 4-6-2	11.18	ST PANCRAS
11.11 HAWICK	11.30	B1 4-6-0	11.35	EDINBURGH
		C15 4-4-2T	11.38	KELSO
		J36 0-6-0	12.05	Melrose
10.30 Portobello		K3 2-6-0	12/18	Carlisle Canal
11.35 Hawick	12.10	J37 0-6-0	12.20	Niddrie
01.00 Aberdeen	12.44	K3 2-6-0	(13.23)	
12.05 EDINBURGH	13.10	A3 4-6-2	13.15	CARLISLE
(01.00 Aberdeen)		K3 2-6-0	13.23	Carlisle Canal
		J35 0-6-0	13.30	Kelso
13.30 Melrose	13.44	J36 0-6-0		
10.40 Carlisle Canal		K3 2-6-0	13/47	Niddrie
12.30 Jedburgh	13.55	J35 0-6-0		
11.35 Carlisle Canal		K3 2-6-0	14/38	Aberdeen
14.21 KELSO	14.45	C15 4-4-2T		
13.26 CARLISLE	15.09	A3 4-6-2	15.13	EDINBURGH
13.30 Niddrie	15.13	K3 2-6-0	15.18	Carlisle Canal
13.50 Tweedmouth	15.39	J39 0-6-0		
14.33 EDINBURGH	15.46	A3 4-6-2	15.51	CARLISLE
		C15 4-4-2T	16.05	BERWICK
16.15 HAWICK	16.37	D30 4-4-0		
		J39 0-6-0	16.55	Tweedmouth
15.28 BERWICK	16.56	G5 0-4-4T		
14.55 Niddrie		K3 2-6-0	16/59	Carlisle Canal
13.35 Carlisle Canal		K3 2-6-0	17/02	Niddrie
		D30 4-4-0	17.15	HAWICK
15.37 CARLISLE	17.36	B1 4-6-0	17.40	EDINBURGH
16.10 EDINBURGH	17.37	B1 4-6-0	17.41	HAWICK
17.45 Galashiels	18.08	J36 0-6-0		
16.35 Niddrie		J36 0-6-0	18/15	Carlisle Canal
08.50 ST PANCRAS	18.14	A3 4-6-2	18.17	EDINBURGH
14.35 Carlisle Canal		K3 2-6-0	18/32	Edinburgh (Meadows)
17.15 Jedburgh	18.40	J35 0-6-0		
		J36 0-6-0	18.48	Galashiels
17.53 EDINBURGH	19.03	A3 4-6-2	19.06	CARLISLE
18.40 Hawick	19.09	J37 0-6-0		(Fwd at 19.20)
		G5 0-4-4T	19.15	BERWICK
		J35 0-6-0	19.17	Carlisle Canal
(18.40 ex Hawick)		J37 0-6-0	19.20	Portobello
16.00 Carlisle Canal		K3 2-6-0	19/51	Niddrie
18.40 BERWICK	20.15	C15 4-4-2T		
19.02 EDINBURGH	20.26	B1 4-6-0	20.29	HAWICK
		J35 0-6-0	20.55	Niddrie
19.33 CARLISLE	21.11	A3 4-6-2	21.15	EDINBURGH
19.27 Portobello	21.14	K3 2-6-0	(22.25)	
15.55 Dundee West		V2 2-6-2	21/41	Carlisle Canal
17.50 Carlisle Canal		K3 2-6-0	21/56	Aberdeen
20.50 Edinburgh (W)		V2 2-6-2	22/12	Carlisle Canal
(19.27 Portobello)		K3 2-6-0	22.25	Carlisle Canal
21.53 EDINBURGH		A3 4-6-2	22/59	ST PANCRAS
22.15 EDINBURGH	23.27	A4 4-6-2	23.31	CARLISLE
20.45 Carlisle Canal		K3 2-6-0	23/42	Niddrie

ST BOSWELLS BRANCH COACHING SETS (1938)

2: BRAKE THIRD/COMPOSITE

St Boswells	06.20	
06.41 Kelso	07.35	
07.57 St Boswells	08.37	att to 08.15 ex Hawick
09.49 Edinburgh	ECS	
ECS Corstorphine	14.51	
Edinburgh	16.10	
17.46 St Boswells	17.55	
18.20 Kelso	18.38	
19.36 Berwick		
Berwick	08.08	
08.31 Reston	08.33	
10.38 St Boswells	11.18	
12.48 Reston	12.52	
13.14 Berwick	15.07	
15.33 Reston	15.36	
16.36 St Boswells	17.55	
19.42 Reston	19.59	
20.18 Duns		

2: BRAKE THIRD/COMPOSITE

Duns	07.06	
07.52 St Boswells	08.35	
08.58 Kelso	10.11	
10.35 St Boswells	10.49	08.48 ex Carlisle
11.55 Edinburgh	14.20	
15.21 St Boswells	15.40	
16.02 Kelso	16.12	
16.36 St Boswells	16.39	
16.51 Galashiels	ECS	
ECS St Boswells		
St Boswells	08.38	
10.16 Reston	10.19	
10.41 Berwick	12.45	
13.15 Reston	13.17	
14.22 St Boswells	15.36	
17.06 Reston	18.44	
19.45 St Boswells	(06.20)	

2: BRAKE THIRD/COMPOSITE

St Boswells	06.20
07.00 Kelso	07.06
07.50 Berwick	17.25
18.20 Kelso	18.27
18.50 St Boswells	19.07
19.31 Kelso	19.50
20.12 St Boswells	(06.20)

2: BRAKE THIRD/COMPOSITE

Craigentinny	01.00	ECS
01.15 Waverley	10.03	Thames- Forth'
11.08 St Boswells	11.17	
11.40 Kelso	14.06	
14.24 St Boswells	14.33	
14.46 Galashiels	14.58	09.15 ex Leeds
15.43 Waverley	17.24	Extra Third n/corr
17.50 Gorebridge	18.07	Extra Third n/corr
18.31 Waverley	ECS	
Craigentinny	(01.00)	

The arrangements for the working of both lines were more complicated that one might expect with the carriage sets for the Berwick trains following a four day cycle which included two workings from Kelso to Edinburgh and back. (It will be noted that one of these, the 16.10 from Waverley, actually ran through to Berwick via St Boswells and Kelso).

A fifth set shuttled between St Boswells and Kelso whilst a sixth was Edinburgh-based and worked between the Waverley and Kelso by being attached to the 10.03 'Thames-Forth Express' Edinburgh to St Pancras as far as St Boswells - probably one of the last instances of an Anglo-Scottish train including non-corridor stock in its formation - and returning from Kelso in time to be coupled to the 09.15 Leeds - Edinburgh express at St Boswells. Upon reaching Edinburgh, the two non-corridor vehicles were separated from the Leeds coaches: the local set being strengthened with a non-corridor third to work an evening rush-hour train to Gorebridge while the main line coaches returned south with the 17.45 Edinburgh to Leeds and Bristol.

Arguably the most notable of these arrangements was that of the Kelso coaches which were attached to the southbound St Pancras express and one wonders what made the railway give such treatment to a town with a population of barely four thousand. It is a feature that history seems to have missed.

Coal traffic was a major feature of the North British Railway which served no less than 114 collieries, 26 being located in the immediate Edinburgh district alone. To cater for this traffic, the NBR constructed a large fleet of 0-6-0 tender engines (292 were handed over to British Railways together with 59 LNER J38 and J39 0-6-0's) which ranged from the smaller J35 (3F) and J36 (2F) classes to the mighty 5F J37 class. The Waverley route did not see a great deal of colliery work; its only pits were located at Hardengreen and Gorebridge and were served by untimetabled trip workings based on Hardengreen and organised by the Controller. There was also a pair of mines situated on the Peebles branch and these too were served by trips from Hardengreen which, with its main line banking commitments, was one of the more important locations on the line. J36 0-6-0 65327 of St Margarets passes Niddrie South Junction with a trip of mineral empties for Hardengreen in June 1961. (W.S.Sellar)

J37 64582 of St Margarets was one of 104 large 5F 0-6-0's that enjoyed the distinction of being the most powerful 0-6-0's in Britain. Although having a route availability of RA8, the utility of the class was such that arrangements had been made for it to run in the Edinburgh district with much the same availability as a J36 with the result that there were very few lines upon which the J37 could not run. 64582 is seen in October 1955 near Niddrie North Junction on the Lothian Lines system heading towards Wanton Walls Junction and the East Coast main line with a service from Meadows Yard, Edinburgh.

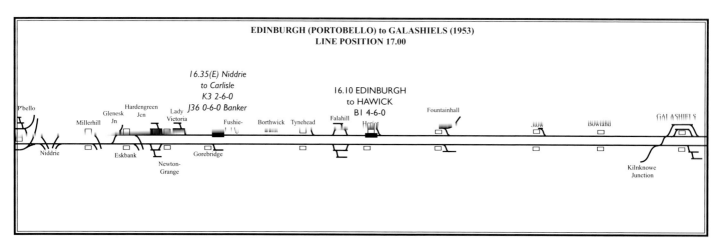

CONTROLLER'S LOG: Although the rush-hour is in full swing three miles away in Edinburgh, there is precious little sign of it south of Portobello where the nightly exodus of office-workers has to be satisfied by no more than a pair of trains.   The first of these is the 16.10 to Hawick which is currently standing at Heriot and the second will be the V3-worked 17.10 Edinburgh to Galashiels.   The two trains account for most season-ticket travel on the line and those who turn up at the Waverley

banked uphill through Gorebridge - is only eight minutes slower than the 16.10 passenger between Hardengreen and Hawick.

The place for activity at the moment is St Boswells where a Tweedmouth 0-4-4T has just arrived with the 15.28 ex Berwick on Tweed and is waiting for the 14.55 Niddrie to Carlisle to clear the station so that it can be shunted over to the up side and leave the down main free for the approaching 13.35 Carlisle Canal to Niddrie.   The up loop is occupied by the

- that cannot be taken in the usual class E trains. The difference between an E and an H is considerable and whereas the former needs one hundred and twenty-seven minutes to run from Carlisle to Hawick, the latter requires thirty minutes more and if the 16.00 were allowed to keep to the main line at Newcastleton, the delay to the Thames-Forth would be in the region of forty minutes.

Since it is the route's most celebrated train it is difficult to resist the impulse to look over

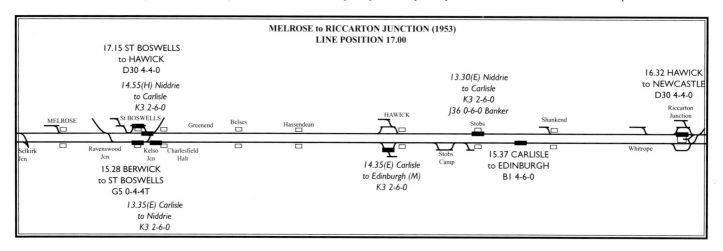

after 17.10 have a wait of almost two hours for another stopping train.   The intervening 17.53 is of only limited use since it runs non-stop to Stow and does not therefore cater for local passengers.

Matters are scarcely any better on the parallel Peebles route where departures are confined to the 17.05 to Galashiels, the 17.27 to Rosewell and the 18.26 to Bonnyrigg.

The paucity of trains is no symptom of post-war austerity since the timetable has changed but little since the golden days of the LNER.   A fact to be savoured is that the 16.35 Niddrie to Carlisle class E goods - now being

17.15 local service to Hawick, its D30 and the adjacent G5 exuding a fairly solid pre-grouping atmosphere.

Matters are also fairly busy at the English end of the route where the down Thames-Forth - in its eighth hour of travel and with its third engine - is crossing the border.   The need for a clear run goes without saying and Newcastleton is reminded to shunt the 16.00 Carlisle - Niddrie goods in the down refuge until the express has passed.   The 16.00 is a class H (almost the lowest and slowest class of goods trains) which clears Carlisle of the dross - generally wagons fitted with grease as opposed to oil axleboxes

the shoulder of the East Coast Controller's shoulder to see how his principal East Coast train - the Flying Scotsman - is running.   It and its Haymarket A4 is booked to cross the border at 16.38 and be in Edinburgh at five-fifty while the Thames-Forth still has ninety miles and the hardest part of its journey ahead of it.

The engine of the Thames-Forth is the same A3 Pacific that worked the up train from Edinburgh to Carlisle earlier in the day.   Based at Carlisle Canal, it will return south during the night after taking over the 22.05 Dundee West - Carlisle express goods at Niddrie from a Haymarket A2 Pacific.

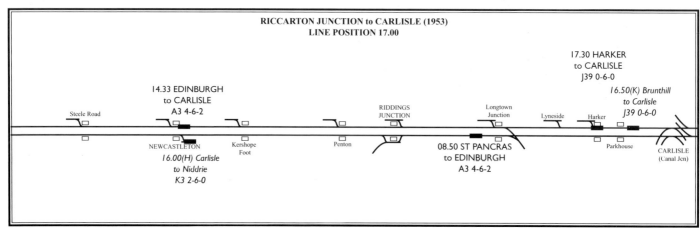

B1 4-6-0 61244 'Strang Steel' passes Falahill with the 12.00 (Saturdays only) Hawick - Edinburgh Waverley. (W.S.Sellar)

One of the great curiosities of the Waverley route was the 10-mile Lauder Light Railway which ran between Fountainhall and Lauder.   Restricted to a 12-tons axleload, it could only be used by RA1 locomotives which had the range to cover the twenty-two miles from Galashiels to Lauder.   When the North British D41 4-4-0 tanks were withdrawn a few years after the grouping, F7 2-4-2T's had to be imported from the Great Eastern and when these in turn had to be replaced twenty years later the LNER looked again to the Great Eastern and transferred half a dozen J67 0-6-0 tank engines to Edinburgh St Margarets.   Two of which were out-based at Galashiels for working the Lauder service but because they lacked the water capacity for the return trip, the curious step was taken of coupling them to redundant tenders to produce a unique hybrid of an engine.   The J67's were eventually replaced by LMS 2MT 2-6-0 during the early 1950's.   68492 shunts its train in Galashiels yard on the 9th September 1950 after working the 09.26 Galashiels to Lauder and the 12.15 return.

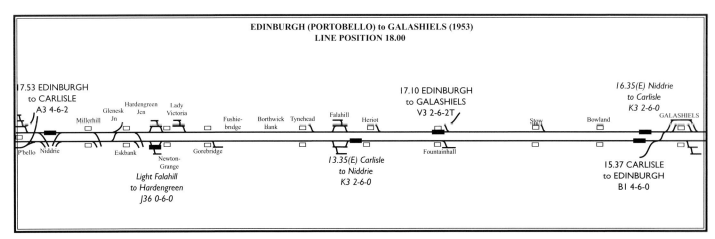

EDINBURGH (PORTOBELLO) to GALASHIELS (1953)
LINE POSITION 18.00

CONTROLLER'S LOG: As has been remarked upon before, V3 2-6-2 tanks are not the most common engines to be seen on the route and where they are seen, it is usually on the short section between Galashiels and Kilknowe Junction when working to and from the Peebles direction. There are three services daily from Edinburgh by this route and four from Galashiels, the imbalance being caused by the 17.10 ex Waverley which runs out via Falahill and back via Peebles.

The 17.10 is the last hope for season-ticket

traffic is transferred in sacks at Carlisle for the 15.30 Aberdeen - Euston.

The engine working the train is the Canal A3 which went down this morning with the 09.25 Carlisle - Edinburgh and will, after terminating at Carlisle, work back to Edinburgh with the 01.10 Canal - Dundee fitted goods.

The supply of banking engines can be a head-ache from time to time especially at Riccarton Junction where only one engine is available to assist trains over Whitrope bank from Newcastleton. The J36 0-6-0 banker is

to be at Newcastleton just as the banker arrives back from its previous working. When the loops and refuge sidings are full, a goods train can always be 'put across the road' (ie. shunted onto the up main line) although to do this, a lull in southbound traffic is required.

A second banking engine seems an obvious solution but Riccarton shed, alas, is no Gateshead or Kingmoor and the chances of getting an engine in a hurry are minimal and usually one has to do the best one can with the booked engine.

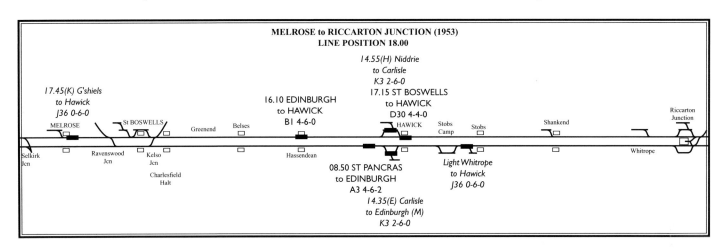

MELROSE to RICCARTON JUNCTION (1953)
LINE POSITION 18.00

holders until the 19.02 Edinburgh to Hawick and the 17.53 ex Edinburgh which has just passed Portobello, runs as an express and does not stop until reaching Stow. This was once a train of some substance since in pregrouping days it conveyed a through coach to Bristol which ran via Leeds and Derby. It also conveyed post and parcels traffic which had to connect with the midnight express from Leeds for St Pancras.

Two world wars and a pair of reorganisations later, both the Bristol carriage and the Leeds connection have disappeared while the postal

now assisting the 16.00 Carlisle to Niddrie and since the banking cycle takes about an hour to complete, it can be seen that this one engine effectively controls the flow of trains from Canal Yard to Edinburgh.

However there are times when one train per hour is not enough because the volume of traffic in Canal yard requires a succession of special workings and when this happens you have to live by your wits for the duration of the crisis. By allowing an hour for each banking operation you can stick trains in loops and refuge sidings, bringing them back onto the main line in order

One concession that has eased matters at Whitrope is the fact that the banker is not required to assist trains all the way to the summit but can cease banking at Riccarton Junction, leaving the train engine to manage the remaining two miles unaided. The fact the gradient eases from 1 in 75 to 1 in 91 is of psychological rather than real assistance.

Meanwhile the Thames-Forth continues its way northwards, drawing away from Hawick, allowing the 14.35 Carlisle - Edinburgh Meadows goods, which has been waiting a path for over an hour, the chance to move on.

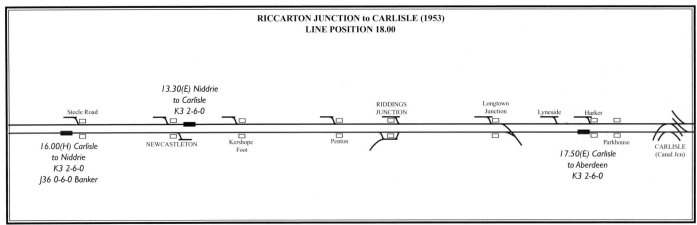

RICCARTON JUNCTION to CARLISLE (1953)
LINE POSITION 18.00

J67 68511 (and tender) on the light railway with the 09.26 Galashiels to Lauder on 26 July 1952.

Working in lieu of the booked V1 2-6-2T, B1 4-6-0 61191 of Edinburgh (St Margarets) arrives in Galashiels on the 19 September 1955 with the 07.55 from Edinburgh via Peebles. This was an unusual working for a 4-6-0 since the four through services on the route were normally handled by a St Margarets V1 2-6-2T but when one of the latter was not available - the St Margarets' V1's suffered from maintenance problems from time to time - a B1 4-6-0 tended to be substituted. The engine went back to Edinburgh with the 10.16 via Peebles and returned later in the day with the 13.18 Edinburgh - Galashiels and the 16.06 Galashiels to Edinburgh. (W.S.Sellar)

In BR days through services to London were limited to the 10.05 and the 21.53 departures from Edinburgh but until 1939 a third express had run at 12.10 from Edinburgh, reaching St Pancras at 21.07. While the timetable proclaimed the midday train to be in every sense the equal of the Thames-Forth and the Night Sleeper, in reality it was a three coach service with a fourth vehicle that was transferred at Carlisle to the 12.10 Glasgow (St Enoch) - St Pancras. Of greater interest was the Pullman dining car which, with its two companion vehicles and the engine, returned to Edinburgh with the midday express from St Pancras. The lightweight formation did not call for a Pacific and the diagrammed engine was a D49 4-4-0. 266 'Lanarkshire' pauses at Galashiels with the 12.10 from Edinburgh during the 1930's.

In postwar days almost all the through trains between Edinburgh and Carlisle were handled by A3 Pacifics and this included several of the stopping services. Double-chimney A3 60043 'Brown Jack' leaves Galashiels with the 14.33 Edinburgh to Carlisle; a service booked to make no less than fourteen intermediate stops. The use of A3's on stopping (parliamentary) trains was by no means confined to the Waverley route and most of the stopping trains between Kings Cross and Grantham were worked by Pacifics. (W.S.Sellar)

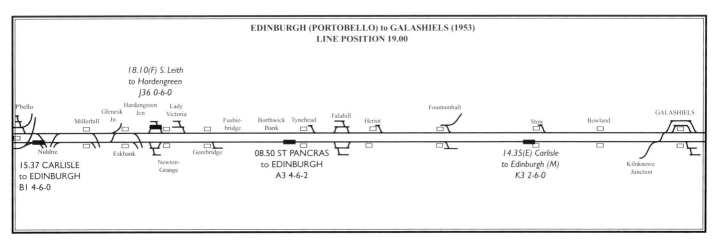

EDINBURGH (PORTOBELLO) to GALASHIELS (1953)
LINE POSITION 19.00

18.10(F) S. Leith
to Hardengreen
J36 0-6-0

P'bello · Millerhill · Glenesk Jn · Hardengreen Jcn · Lady Victoria · Fushiebridge · Borthwick Bank · Tynehead · Falahill · Heriot · Fountainhall · Stow · Bowland · GALASHIELS

Niddrie · Eskbank · Newton Grange · Gorebridge · Kilnknowe Junction

15.37 CARLISLE
to EDINBURGH
B1 4-6-0

08.50 ST PANCRAS
to EDINBURGH
A3 4-6-2

14.35(E) Carlisle
to Edinburgh (M)
K3 2-6-0

CONTROLLER'S LOG: More than ten hours after leaving London, the Thames-Forth approaches the lights of Edinburgh and journey's end. After arriving in the Waverley, the stock will be taken to Craigentinny for tomorrow's 10.05 departure while the engine will be turned and coaled on Haymarket loco before returning south with the 22.05 Dundee West - Carlisle express goods.

The central part of the district, Galashiels

involved in marshalling goods trains since in common with most services it has to be made up in distinct sections to simplify matters when it arrives in Edinburgh. In this instance the various parts are: engine, mineral empties and dock traffic for Hardengreen, livestock for stations between Ratho and Glasgow, livestock for Edinburgh and stations north of Inverkeithing and, at the rear of the train, general goods for Niddrie, Edinburgh and the

the 18.40 and transferred to the 20.55.

Passenger activity south of Galashiels continues to sport a strong pre-grouping flavour. A NER G5 0-4-4T waits to depart for Berwick from St Boswells after connecting with the up express while a D30 4-4-0 calls at Riccarton Junction with a Newcastle - Hawick service. A few months ago an NBR D31 4-4-0 could be added to the tally, 62281 once being the regular engine on the 18.13 Carlisle to

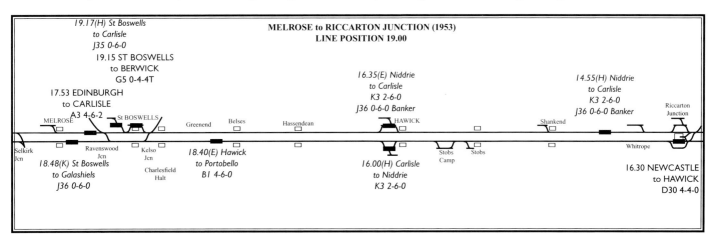

MELROSE to RICCARTON JUNCTION (1953)
LINE POSITION 19.00

19.17(H) St Boswells
to Carlisle
J35 0-6-0

19.15 ST BOSWELLS
to BERWICK
G5 0-4-4T

17.53 EDINBURGH
to CARLISLE
A3 4-6-2

16.35(E) Niddrie
to Carlisle
K3 2-6-0
J36 0-6-0 Banker

14.55(H) Niddrie
to Carlisle
K3 2-6-0
J36 0-6-0 Banker

MELROSE · St BOSWELLS · Greenend · Belses · Hassendean · HAWICK · Shankend · Riccarton Junction

Selkirk Jcn · Ravenswood Jcn · Kelso Jcn · Charlesfield Halt · Stobs Camp · Stobs · Whitrope

18.48(K) St Boswells
to Galashiels
J36 0-6-0

18.40(E) Hawick
to Portobello
B1 4-6-0

16.00(H) Carlisle
to Niddrie
K3 2-6-0

16.30 NEWCASTLE
to HAWICK
D30 4-4-0

to Hawick, can hardly be described as an industrial area yet it produces sufficient traffic to warrant a surprising number of originating goods trains.

St Boswells is something of a central figure in this respect and is busy with traffic that has arrived in the last few hours from Greenlaw, Jedburgh, the Tweedmouth branch and Galashiels, all of which is shunted to form the 19.17 goods to Carlisle and the 20.55 to Niddrie.

The traffic conveyed is quite varied and ranges from general goods to livestock and mineral empties. The 20.55 St Boswells to Niddrie is a good example of the complications

NB main line to Dundee. Each of the sections have to be marshalled in strict station order and thus four sidings alone - one for each section - are required for making up the train. It explains how it is that even at small yards such as St Boswells', the shunting is almost continuous and in fact the yard pilot is on duty from 04.00 until 22.45.

The 20.55 ex St Boswells is closely linked with the 18.40 Hawick to Portobello which has just passed Belses. The 18.40 is primarily a Glasgow service and calls at St Boswells to collect any Cadder traffic that may have come in during the day. At the same time any Edinburgh traffic from Hawick is removed from

Riccarton Junction. Latterly the train has been diagrammed to a Canal D49 4-4-0 which returns light to Carlisle from Riccarton Junction.

Postwar modernity is heralded by 4MT 2-6-0 43139 as it heads towards Carlisle with the last Langholm train of the day. Optimistically intended to be a replacement for the standard LMS 4F 0-6-0, it is interesting to find one working a diagram that used to be covered by a J39 0-6-0 from the opposing camp although, given that the J39 was a class 5 engine, it does not seem that modernisation provided much of a benefit in this case. The J39-hauled train preceding 43139 is the daily goods trip from Blackbank sidings at Gretna Green.

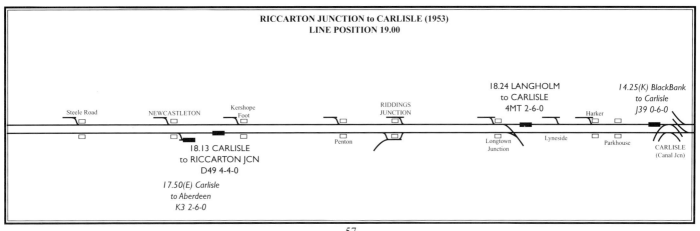

RICCARTON JUNCTION to CARLISLE (1953)
LINE POSITION 19.00

18.24 LANGHOLM
to CARLISLE
4MT 2-6-0

14.25(K) BlackBank
to Carlisle
J39 0-6-0

Steele Road · NEWCASTLETON · Kershope Foot · RIDDINGS JUNCTION · Harker · CARLISLE (Canal Jcn)

Penton · Longtown Junction · Lyneside · Parkhouse

18.13 CARLISLE
to RICCARTON JCN
D49 4-4-0

17.50(E) Carlisle
to Aberdeen
K3 2-6-0

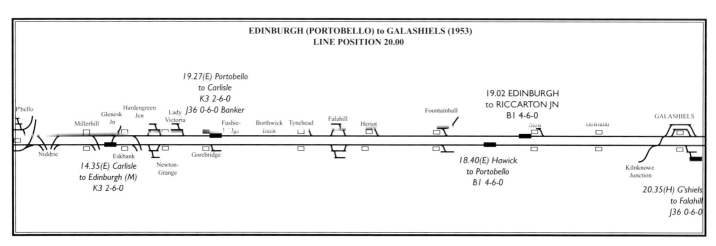

EDINBURGH (PORTOBELLO) to GALASHIELS (1953)
LINE POSITION 20.00

CONTROLLER'S LOG: In days gone by the evening Carlisle to Edinburgh passenger - now approaching Kershope Foot - was the second of two afternoon expresses from St Pancras.

Up to 1914 it departed from London at 13.30 and running via Leicester, Trent and Sheffield, left Leeds at 17.37 to reach Carlisle at 19.53 where the Edinburgh section was attached to the 20.02 North British express which terminated in

Euston, connecting with 19.33 from Carlisle and arriving in Edinburgh at 22.25: a journey fifteen minutes slower than it had been in 1914 although it must be said that Edinburgh passengers who change at Carstairs instead of Carlisle can arrive in Princes Street at 21.40.

Those who choose to change at Carlisle have the consolation of making the 409-mile trip behind both LMS and LNER Pacifics.

Hawick, which is seldom free from freight

train - it will not reach Craiginches until 09.00 tomorrow - and is designed to connect with the 14,40 goods from Kittybrewster which runs to most stations on the Great North.

Watching the 17.53 Edinburgh - Carlisle slow for its Newcastleton stop, one wonders if there will be any difficulties with passengers tonight. The train runs non-stop from Newcastleton to Longtown Junction but a footnote in the timetable states that passengers

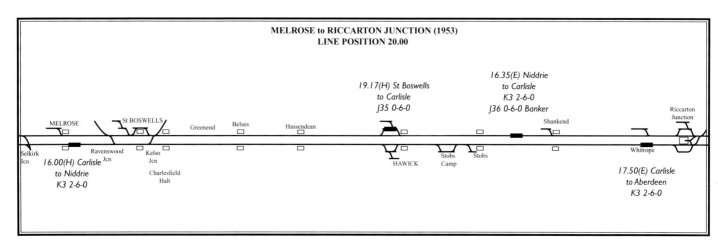

MELROSE to RICCARTON JUNCTION (1953)
LINE POSITION 20.00

Edinburgh at 22.25 after making the usual stops at Hawick, Melrose and Galashiels.

The 13.30 did not survive the Great War but the midday express remained, leaving St Pancras at 12.00 and transferring its Edinburgh coach to the 18.28 from Carlisle to reach Edinburgh at 21.01. The final leg of the journey was completed in the company of the Pullman dining car which had worked up to Carlisle in the 12.10 from Edinburgh.

Nowadays the only through Midland services are the Thames-Forth and the night sleeper and those who wish to do the journey on LMS metals during the afternoon are obliged to use the 13.15 Mid-day Scot from

trains waiting to exchange crews, is for once almost silent. The evening St Boswells to Carlisle goods is in the yard attaching traffic but otherwise all is quiet.

The last exchange took place half an hour ago with the trains concerned now passing Melrose and Stobs respectively whilst the next down train, the 17.50 Canal to Aberdeen, is one of a minority that is relieved at Hawick in the normal way by the St Margarets crew who bring in the 19.02 passenger from Edinburgh.

The 17.50 goods is remarkable in that it conveys traffic for Aberdeen and the North only and is composed very largely of traffic for the Great North of Scotland system. It is not a fast

for Riddings Junction and the Langholm branch may travel via Longtown Junction.

The generous intent of the facility is somewhat leavened by the fact that to take advantage of it involves a wait of no less than thirteen hours at Longtown. Charity in the border regions can be an elastic proposition at times.

Running ahead of the 17.53 is a 4-4-0 running light to Carlisle. This - usually a D49 - is the engine that worked down with the 18.13 from Carlisle and is hardly a shining example of exemplary locomotive utilisation. It is however a useful asset when one is short of power at Riccarton Junction!

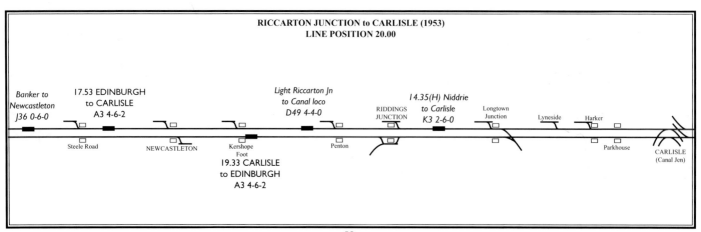

RICCARTON JUNCTION to CARLISLE (1953)
LINE POSITION 20.00

Winters could be savage over the Cheviots and as a precaution against drifts Hawick shed was obliged to maintain an engine with snow ploughs as a matter of routine. Other engines were fitted as judgement decreed and J36 0-6-0 65327 of St Margaret's was selected as one of the engines on 8th February 1958, during a winter that was little different from any other. Although a St Margaret's engine, 65327 was out-based at Galashiels and was about to depart on the Peebles goods diagram. The involved working the 12.15 Galashiels to Peebles, the 15.00 Peebles to Hardengreen Junction and the 19.00 back to Peebles where the engine stabled for the night. The following day the engine worked the 09.20 Peebles to Galashiels where it was exchanged for another engine. (W.S.Sellar)

The twenty-four D30 4-4-0's of 1914 were well scattered throughout the North British but by the 1950's only Thornton Junction and Hawick sheds had them in appreciable numbers; the greatest concentration (eight) being at the latter where they dominated local services until the end of 1958. 62432 'Quentin Durward' of Hawick leaves Melrose with a local train for Galashiels on 15th May 1958. (W.S.Sellar)

D30 4-4-0 62432 'Quentin Durward' stands in Melrose yard prior to working the 13.30 goods to St Boswells on 16th May 1958. In spite of their passenger status the Hawick D30's were often used locally as mixed traffic engines. (W.S.Sellar)

Hawick marked both the halfway point between Edinburgh and Carlisle and the start of the climb to Whitrope summit: eleven miles at an average of 1 in 89 for which the booking of twenty-four and a half minutes - 26 mph - was by no means excessive. Carlisle Canal A3 60079 'Bayardo' restarts the 17.53 Edinburgh - Carlisle from Hawick on the 1 April 1958. (W.S.Sellar)

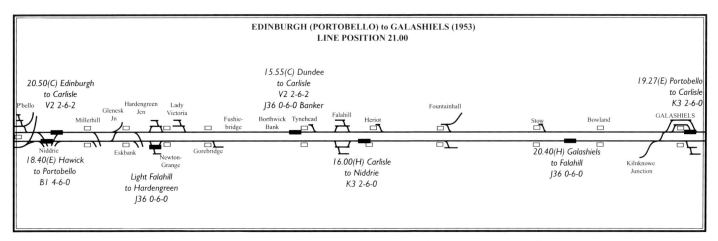

EDINBURGH (PORTOBELLO) to GALASHIELS (1953)
LINE POSITION 21.00

CONTROLLER'S LOG: As darkness starts to cloak the borders, preparations are made for the night shift which consists very largely of goods operations. A pair of passenger trains will leave Edinburgh for Carlisle in about an hour's time but otherwise the goods service will have the line to themselves.

Planning the night services includes booking up the night trains, a procedure that involves agreeing with the receiving point the loads to be taken on each service before the trains are made up in the yards.

discussed. Equally they might ask for a train to be made up entirely of LNW traffic to be run as a special to Crewe and be re-engined and remanned at Carlisle. Similarly, if there is a shortfall of Midland traffic and a glut of loading for Whitehaven, one might consider making up a complete section for the Furness instead of one for the Midland.

The same applies in the opposite direction; the Carlisle Controller reeling off his list of trains and proposed loads which we reach agreement over. The motive power position is

suburban line. The engine change takes place at Haymarket.

The formation of both trains is the same - engine, Upperby, Durran Hill and Canal roughs - but the 20.50 from Edinburgh conveys a single engine load and does not need to take a banker at either Hardengreen or Hawick.

To say that people spring to attention as a Class C goes by is only a slight exaggeration but delays to them are certainly followed as zealously as those for express passenger trains and the train to watch carefully is the

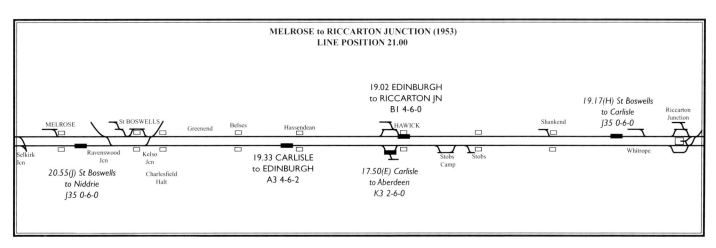

MELROSE to RICCARTON JUNCTION (1953)
LINE POSITION 21.00

Most southbound goods services run in sections made up, typically, of about 20 wagons for the LNW on the engine, 20 for the Midland in the centre of the train and 20 'roughs' for Carlisle (ie Maryport & Carlisle, Furness, North Eastern etc) on the brake and one of the reasons for 'agreeing' loads is to give Carlisle notice of the traffic that is coming its way.

If, for example, there was a blockage in Upperby Yard that looked as though it was going to be prolonged, the possibility of leaving LNW loads off the trains from Edinburgh and replacing them with Midland traffic might be

checked to make sure that engines of the correct type are marked up for each working and that guards, drivers and firemen have been allocated to each turn of duty.

A pair of trains of quite a special nature has made an appearance at the north end of the section, these being class C express goods which except for fish is the highest and most urgent category of goods train. Both are booked to 'Green Arrow' V2 2-6-2's and are worked through to Carlisle by their crews. The Dundee train is unusual in that it is routed through Edinburgh Waverley and not the

19.27 Portobello to Carlisle goods which - if everything is going to plan - will go inside at St Boswells until the two class C's have passed.

Since the traffic conveyed on both expresses is of a high priority, considerable detail of the loads is passed on to the Carlisle Controller who will want to move the Midland and LNW sections forward with his trip engines to Durran Hill and Upperby with the least delay. An appreciable amount of traffic will be for Manchester, Liverpool and Great Western stations, the latter connecting with the 03.20 Upperby to Crewe (Gresty Lane).

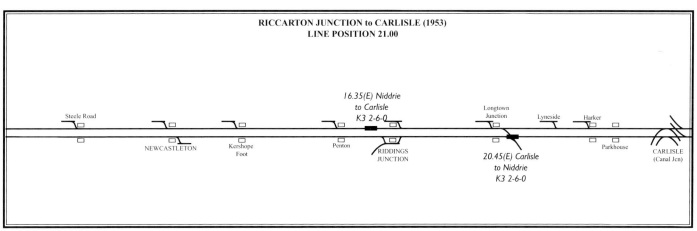

RICCARTON JUNCTION to CARLISLE (1953)
LINE POSITION 21.00

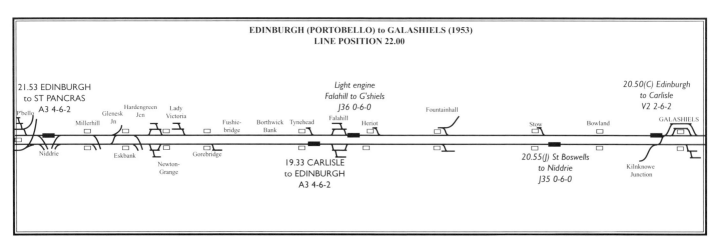

EDINBURGH (PORTOBELLO) to GALASHIELS (1953)
LINE POSITION 22.00

CONTROLLER'S LOG: It is a private opinion but to the writer's mind the up train skirting the junctions at Niddrie is far and away the best way of travelling overnight between the two capitals.

Eighteen shillings and sixpence - plus an extra ten shillings for the attendant at quiet times to ensure a compartment to oneself - is by no means a steep price to pay for the luxury of lying in bed watching the lights of the passing stations pass by - the injunction to draw the blind is ignored - until drifting off to sleep as the Pacific gathers speed on the drop from

passengers an additional couple of hours in bed. The luxury of watching from one's bed the 07.05 Kettering - St Pancras being overtaken at Bedford is in itself worth the trip to London.

Thus when on duty there are trains one monitors with especial interest and of these, 16 up - the London sleeper - heads the list. (Another is the train just pulling out of Carlisle since it will accompany us right through the night shift!)

With only eight vehicles - as opposed to the ten of the day train - its A3 Pacific is less likely to lose time on the more severe sections of line

Waverley Goods to Carlisle trains do not change footplates at Hawick and to claim that they are the hardest firing turns in Scotland is no understatement. The crews work back with the 01.10 and 01.30 departures from Carlisle while the engines return to Edinburgh with the 01.30 and the 02.15 workings from Canal. The 01.10 is booked to the A3 Pacific which later works the up Thames-Forth.

The Canal Inspector will have his pilot engines standing by to trip the Midland and LNW sections of the Dundee and Edinburgh trains to Durran Hill and Upperby yards as

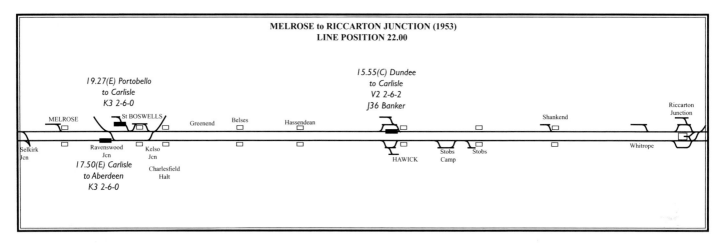

MELROSE to RICCARTON JUNCTION (1953)
LINE POSITION 22.00

Falahill to Galashiels. Carlisle, Skipton, Leeds and Nottingham pass unnoticed and eventually one wakes to savour what is unquestionably the feature that makes this particular train so special. Passengers in every other sleeping car that enters London are obliged to rise, wash, shave and dress at a time and pace commensurate with arriving before the rush hour starts. The Midland, on the other hand, do things in a much more civilised manner by scheduling its sleeping car services to arrive *after* the rush hour; an arrangement that allows

although that does not mean that any chances can be taken. The 20.50 Waverley Goods to Carlisle fully piped goods - one of the few goods trains to be worked through to Carlisle by an Edinburgh crew - is far enough ahead to keep out of harms way but an eye must be kept on the 19.27 Portobello - Carlisle goods which has been shunted at St Boswells for the 20.50 ex Edinburgh which it will follow as far as Hawick where it will go inside for the sleeper and to change crews with the 20.45 Carlisle - Niddrie.

The 15.55 Dundee West and the 20.50

soon as they have arrived and may come as a surprise to learn that traffic is still routed on pre-grouping lines. Wagons from Edinburgh to Birmingham, for example, may not necessarily travel together since those for ex-Midland destinations will go forward in the 05.15 Durran Hill to Birmingham (Washwood Heath) via Leeds whilst those for LNW stations will be taken by the 05.15 Upperby to Wolverhampton (Bushbury). Such segregation may seem ludicrous but the sheer volume of traffic on the move is in itself an obstacle to reform.

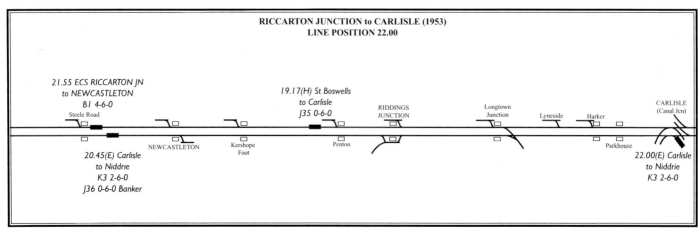

RICCARTON JUNCTION to CARLISLE (1953)
LINE POSITION 22.00

A stranger in the camp. The through workings from Hawick and Riccarton Junction to Newcastle were worked by D30 4-4-0's, one of which stayed overnight in Tyneside in order to work the 05.50 Newcastle to Riccarton Junction. Occasionally the booked engine would fail and Blaydon shed would have to provide a substitute which was usually either a K1 2-6-0 or a D49 4-4-0. From the summer of 1955 Blaydon received a small allocation of BR 4MT 2-6-0's which became frequent if not regular visitors to Hawick on the occasions when Blaydon had to find a replacement for the 05.50 from Newcastle BR Standard 4MT 2-6-0 76049 of Blaydon is seen being prepared on Hawick loco for the 16.32 Hawick - Newcastle after one such rescue.

For many years local passenger services (including the St Boswells - Berwick trains) in the Hawick area relied upon the latter's allocation of five NBR C15 4-4-2 tanks but by the early 1950's the class was in such a poor state of repair that withdrawals commenced in 1954. Provisional replacement included BR and LMS 2-6-4T's, an LNER V1 2-6-2T's and an ex-NBR C16 4-4-2T. The larger of these seem to have been regarded as an extravagence but C16 67495 - seen on Hawick loco in September 1955 - arrived from St Margaret's in April 1955 and remained at Hawick until being withdrawn a year later. It was replaced by 67489 of Dundee which remained in the area until the end of steam. (W.S.Sellar)

With a population of only seventeen thousand, Hawick was not a focal point for passenger traffic but it was an important location in the textile trade and this, together with a flourishing market in cattle, ensured that goods receipts outweighed passenger takings by a considerable margin. The goods workings together with the occasion terminating passenger train made Hawick an interesting point from which to watch trains but its key role lay in the fact it lay half-way between Edinburgh and Carlisle and was the point where the through goods services, of which there was a considerable number, changed footplates. To increase the chances of the changeovers occurring as planned, each train was allowed a minimum of half an hour - and often longer - at Hawick.

Changeovers were not the only operational difficulty presented by Hawick since the line to the south rose almost 650 feet - an average gradient of 1 in 89 - in the ten miles to Whitrope Summit which meant that almost every goods train had to have banking assistance before setting out for Carlisle. A pair of J36 0-6-0's were employed on the banking duties, each cycle taking approximately an hour.

As can be seen from the table below, for all its remoteness, there were not many hours in the day when Hawick was quiet.

TRAFFIC WORKING : HAWICK (1953)

Train	Arr		Comments	Dep	Destination
243: 22.15 Edinburgh	23.46	A4 4-6-2		**00.00**	**Carlisle : 01.10**
529: 22.00 Carlisle Canal	00.07	K3 2-6-0			(Fwd at 01.20)
(558: 19.27 Portobello)		K3 plus J36 Banker		00.15	Carlisle (Canal): 02.04
502: 23.15 Falahill	00.54	J37 0-6-0	Terminate		
(529: 22.00 Carlisle Canal)		K3 2-6-0		01.20	Portobello (04.02)
Light engine ex Whitrope	01.20	J36 0-6-0			
3: 23.10 Carlisle Canal	01.30	J35 0-6-0		01.55	St Boswells (02.28)
768: 02.34 Carlisle Canal	02.34	A3 4-6-2		02.45	Dundee (07.30)
625: 22.05 Dundee West		A3 4-6-2		02.46	Carlisle (Canal): 04.04
767: 01.30 Carlisle Canal	02.54	V2 2-6-2		03.05	Perth North : 07.20
528: 00.10 Carlisle Canal	03.17	A3 4-6-2	C/over with 569		(Fwd at 03.50)
569: 20.20 Aberdeen	03.28	K3 2-6-0	C/over with 528		(Fwd at 03.55)
(528: 00.17 Carlisle Canal)		A3 4-6-2		03.50	Niddrie (05.54)
(569: 20.20 Aberdeen)		K3 plus J36 Banker		03.55	Carlisle (Canal) : 05.19
509: 00.55 Inverkeithing	04.02	K3 2-6-0	C/over with 618		(Fwd at 04.35)
618: 02.15 Carlisle Canal	04.22	V2 2-6-2	C/over with 599		(Fwd at 04.42)
(509: 00.55 Inverkeithing)		K3 plus D30 Banker		04.35	Carlisle (Canal): 05.56
(618: 02.15 Carlisle Canal)		V2 2-6-2		04.42	Edinburgh Meadows: 06.55
Light engine ex Whitrope	04.55	J36 0-6-0			
253: 04.08 Carlisle Postal	05.16	A4 4-6-2		**05.29**	**Edinburgh (07.02)**
522: 02.25 Portobello	05.33	D49 4-4-0	Terminate		
227: 04.10 Edinburgh News	05.48	B1 4-6-0	Terminate		
61		D30 4-4-0		**06.15**	**Newcastle (09.11)**
185: 21.05 London (St Pancras)	06.22	A4 4-6-2		**06.27**	**Edinburgh (07.54)**
577: 22.25 Aberdeen	06.35	K3 2-6-0	C/over with 567		(Fwd at 07.05)
217		D49 4-4-0		**06.44**	**Edinburgh (08.37)**
567: 04.20 Carlisle Canal	06.50	K3 2-6-0	C/over with 577		(Fwd at 07.25)
(577: 22.25 Aberdeen)		K3 plus J36 Banker		07.05	Carlisle (Upperby): 09.10
(567: 04.20 Carlisle Canal)		K3 2-6-0		07.25	Portobello (09.29)
523: 05.05 Portobello	07.52	J37 0-6-0	Terminate		
553: 23.05 Dundee	08.03	A3 4-6-2	C/over with 65		(Fwd at 09.05)
Light engine ex Whitrope	08.05	J36 0-6-0			
221		B1 4-6-0		**08.07**	**Edinburgh (09.40)**
656: 06.05 Carlisle Canal	08.17	B1 4-6-0	C/over with 55	08.45	Aberdeen (18.58)
119: 08.00 Newcastleton	08.46	D30 4-4-0	Terminate		
229: 06.35 Edinburgh	08.44	B1 4-6-0		**08.53**	**Carlisle : 10.29**
558		J37 0-6-0		09.00	Portobello (11.58)
(553: 23.05 Dundee)		A3 plus J36 Banker		09.05	Carlisle (Canal): 10.59
651: 00.30 Dundee West	09.36	K3 2-6-0	C/over with 503		(Fwd at 10.20)
503: 08.00 Carlisle Canal	09.54	K3 2-6-0	C/over with 65	10.15	Perth: 17.26
(651: 00.30 Dundee West)		K3 plus J36 Banker		10.20	Carlisle (Canal): 12.14
Light engine ex Whitrope	10.25	J36 0-6-0			
230: 08.35 Edinburgh	10.26	B1 4-6-0	Terminate		
13: 07.00 Carlisle Canal	10.30	J39 0-6-0	Terminate		
227: 09.05 Carlisle	10.46	A3 4-6-2		**10.52**	**Edinburgh (12.20)**
228		B1 4-6-0		**11.11**	**Edinburgh (13.11)**
521		J37 0-6-0		11.35	Niddrie (15.18)
132: 10.05 Edinburgh	11.33	A3 4-6-2		**11.37**	**London (St Pancras): 20.45**
Light engine ex Whitrope	11.40	J36 0-6-0			

Train	Arr		Comments	Dep	Destination
108		J39 0-6-0		11.45	Carlisle (Canal): 16.35
600: 10.40 Carlisle Canal	12.38	K3 2-6-0	C/over with 525		(Fwd at 13.20)
525: 10.30 Portobello	12.44	K3 2-6-0	C/over with 600		(Fwd at 13.42)
(600: 10.40 Carlisle Canal)		K3 2-6-0		13.20	Niddrie (15.26)
232: 12.05 Edinburgh	13.30	A3 4-6-2		**13.33**	**Carlisle: 14.45**
(525: 10.30 Portobello)		K3 plus J36 Banker		13.42	Carlisle (Canal): 15.36
772: 11.35 Carlisle Canal	13.43	K3 2-6-0	C/over with 539		(Fwd at 14.10)
539: 01.00 Aberdeen	13.52	K3 2-6-0	C/over with 77	14.10	Carlisle (Canal): 16.04
(772: 11.35 Carlisle Canal)		K3 plus J36 Banker		14.10	Aberdeen (01.45)
4862: 11.20 Newcastle	14.15	D30 4-4-0	Terminate		
244: 13.26 Carlisle	14.47	A3 4-6-2		**14.53**	**Edinburgh (16.20)**
Light engine ex Whitrope	15.00	J36 0-6-0			
Light engine ex Whitrope	15.30	J36 0-6-0			
500: 13.30 Niddrie	15.47	K3 2-6-0	C/over with 518		(Fwd at 16.45)
518: 13.35 Carlisle Canal	16.00	K3 2-6-0	C/over with 500		(Fwd at 16.35)
235: 14.35 Edinburgh	16.06	A3 4-6-2		**16.14**	**Carlisle: 17.52**
117		D30 4-4-0		16.15	St Boswells (16.37)
177		D30 4-4-0		16.32	Newcastle (20.00)
(518: 13.35 Carlisle Canal)		K3 2-6-0		16.35	Niddrie (16.39)
594: 14.35 Carlisle Canal	16.42	K3 2-6-0	C/over with 537		(Fwd at 18.05)
(500: 13.30 Niddrie)		K3 plus J36 Banker		16.45	Carlisle (Canal): 18.39
250: 15.37 Carlisle	17.10	B1 4-6-0		**17.16**	**Edinburgh (19.08)**
537: 14.55 Niddrie	17.30	K3 2-6-0	C/over with 594		(Fwd at 18.05)
140: 17.15 St Boswells	17.42	D30 4-4-0	Terminate		
71: 08.50 London (St Pancras)	17.52	A3 4-6-2		**17.58**	**Edinburgh (19.22)**
(537: 14.55 Niddrie)		K3 plus J36 Banker		18.05	Carlisle (Canal): 20.26
(594: 14.35 Carlisle Canal)		K3 2-6-0		18.05	Edinburgh Meadows: 20.25
Light engine ex Whitrope	18.05	J36 0-6-0			
237: 16.10 Edinburgh	18.08	B1 4-6-0	Terminate		
506		B1 4-6-0		18.40	Portobello: 21.03
517: 16.35 Niddrie	18.41	K3 2-6-0	C/over with 504		(Fwd at 19.35)
504: 16.00 Carlisle Canal	18.56	K3 2-6-0	C/over with 51	19.15	Niddrie : 21.50
239: 17.53 Edinburgh	19.21	A3 4-6-2		**19.26**	**Carlisle (20.40)**
4896: 16.30 Newcastle	19.27	D30 4-4-0	Terminate		
(517: 16.35 Niddrie)		K3 plus J36 Banker		19.35	Carlisle (Canal): 21.29
Light engine ex Whitrope	19.35	J36 0-6-0			
86: 19.17 St Boswells	19.51	J35 0-6-0		20.00	Carlisle (Canal): 22.40
612: 17.50 Carlisle Canal	20.29	K3 2-6-0			(Fwd at 21.29)
271: 19.33 Carlisle	20.49	A3 4-6-2		**20.55**	**Edinburgh (22.25)**
240: 19.02 Edinburgh	20.52	B1 4-6-0		**21.20**	**Riccarton Jcn (21.48)**
Light engine ex Whitrope	20.55	J36 0-6-0			
(612: 17.50 Carlisle Canal)		K3 2-6-0		21.29	Aberdeen: 09.00
575: 15.55 Dundee West	22.01	V2 plus J36 Banker		22.20	Carlisle (Canal): 23.41
557: 20.50 Edinburgh	22.32	V2 2-6-2		22.45	Carlisle (Canal): 00.06
617: 20.45 Carlisle Canal	22.52	K3 2-6-0	C/over with 558		(Fwd at 23.15)
558: 19.27 Portobello	22.54	K3 2-6-0	C/over with 617		(Fwd at 00.15)
(617: 20.45 Carlisle Canal)		K3 2-6-0		23.15	Niddrie: 01.19
216: 21.53 Edinburgh	23.14	A3 4-6-2		**23.19**	**London (St Pancras): 09.12**
Light engine ex Whitrope	23.20	J36 0-6-0			

HAWICK BANKERS : 1953

J36 0-6-0

Arr	Location	Dep	Train
	Hawick	09.05	23.05 Dundee - Carlisle
10.00	Whitrope Summit	10.05	Light
10.25	Hawick	13.42	10.30 Portobello - Carlisle
14.37	Whitrope Summit	14.40	Light
15.00	Hawick	16.45	13.30 Niddrie - Carlisle
17.40	Whitrope Summit	17.45	Light
18.05	Hawick	19.35	16.35 Niddrie - Carlisle
20.30	Whitrope Summit	20.35	Light
20.55	Hawick	00.15	19.27 Portobello - Carlisle
01.05	Whitrope Summit	01.10	Light
01.20	Hawick	(03.55)	

J36 0-6-0

Arr	Location	Dep	Train
	Hawick	03.55	20.20 Aberdeen - Carlisle
04.30	Whitrope Summit	04.35	Light
04.55	Hawick	07.05	22.25 Aberdeen - Carlisle
07.40	Whitrope Summit	07.45	Light
08.05	Hawick	10.20	00.30 Dundee - Carlisle
11.15	Whitrope Summit	11.20	Light
11.40	Hawick	14.10	01.00 Aberdeen - Carlisle
15.05	Whitrope Summit	15.10	Light
15.30	Hawick	18.05	14.45 Niddrie - Carlisle
19.10	Whitrope Summit	19.15	Light
19.35	Hawick	22.20	15.55 Dundee - Carlisle
22.55	Whitrope Summit	23.00	Light
23.20	Hawick	(09.05)	

Note : 00.55 Inverkeithing - Carlisle (04.35 ex Hawick) banked by D30 4-4-0 en route to Newcastleton.

J36 0-6-0 65316 came to Hawick from Edinburgh (St Margarets) in April 1951 and remained at the shed for seven years before being transferred to Polmont in August 1958. Equipped with a cab shelter for the ten-mile tender-first return run from Whitrope when on banking duties, the engine is seen shunting at Hawick shortly before being reallocated to Polmont. The banking duties are shown in the table to the left. (W.S.Sellar)

North British motive power remained active between Edinburgh and Carlisle right up to the 1960's although it is a matter of regret that the C10 and C11 Atlantics which had worked the principal trains from 1906 disappeared for scrap by 1937, most of their duties being taken over by LNER Pacifics. North British 4-4-0's fared much better and even by the mid-1950's very few had been withdrawn. Two classes of engine - D30 and D34 - remained in use, the former being well represented on the Waverley route with eight examples being allocated to Hawick for local and branch duties. (The remainder of the class was well strewn over the system, the January 1953 allocation of D30's being: Bathgate (1), Dundee (3), Dunfermline (2) St Margaret's (2), Hawick (8), Haymarket (1), Stirling (1) and Thornton Junction (6))

The D34 class was very similar to the D30 in many respects but had smaller driving wheels to give the increased tractive effort needed for mixed traffic duties on steeply graded lines such as the West Highland. In spite of this, the class favoured for the Waverley route was the D30 and it was not until the Spring of 1958 - very late in the day - that D34's were allocated to Hawick as replacements for withdrawn D30's. As it happened the two D34's were the last North British 4-4-0's to be based at Hawick and outlasted the D30's by three years. (D34 allocations in January 1953 were: Bathgate (1), Dundee (1), St Margaret's (7), Thornton Junction (5) and Eastfield (13))

In the upper view one of the two D34's that came to Hawick in February 1958, 62494 'Glen Gour' arrives in Melrose on Friday 16th May 1958 with the 16.15 school train from Galashiels. On the same date, below, D30 62421 'Laird o' Monkbarns passes Melrose with the 18.50 St Boswells - Galashiels local goods: a turn perhaps better suited to one of the smaller-wheeled D34's. (W.S.Sellar)

A4 Pacifics had only one booked duty - the 22.15 Edinburgh - Carlisle and the 04.08 Carlisle - Edinburgh - over the Waverley route and because this ran during the hours of darkness, the working went largely unnoticed.   By 1960 most of the day trains to Kings Cross were - in theory - worked by English Electric Type 4 diesel-electrics, releasing Pacifics other than A3's for Waverley route duties.   On a cold and wintry 2nd of December 1961 A4 60031 'Golden Plover' was employed on the 06.40 Edinburgh - Carlisle stopping train - seen here on the final yards of Whitrope bank - in lieu of the diagrammed B1 4-6-0.   (W.S.Sellar)

Another Pacific discovered taking the place of a smaller engine on 2nd of December 1961 was A3 60068 'Sir Visto' of Carlisle which worked the 08.35 Carlisle (Canal) to Niddrie instead of the usual K3 2-6-0.   The spell of bad weather had probably caused some dislocation of engine workings. (W.S.Sellar)

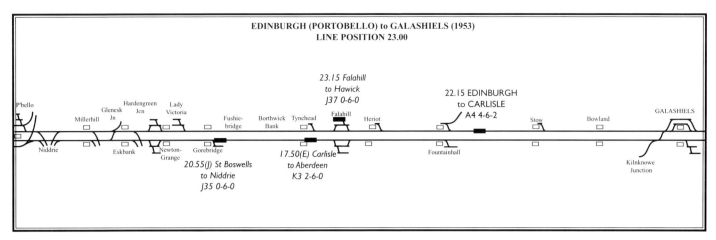

EDINBURGH (PORTOBELLO) to GALASHIELS (1953)
LINE POSITION 23.00

CONTROLLER'S LOG: Aficionados of the LNER are pretty good at telling you which trains are worked by the celebrated A4 Streamliners but there is one working they are almost certain to miss and that is the service presently on the up road climbing Falahill bank: the 22.15 Edinburgh to Carlisle.

The 22.15 is essentially a relief to the 21.53 Edinburgh - St Pancras, running primarily for the benefit of fish and parcels traffic and loading quite heavily - the reason for a class 8 engine

with the 10.10 from Kings Cross.

After reaching Carlisle the A4 is turned and coaled on Canal loco before returning to Edinburgh with the 04.08 parcels from Carlisle and is, under normal circumstances, the only instance of one of the class appearing on the Waverley route. It is not, though, the only Haymarket engine to visit both Newcastle and Carlisle in the same day since the Haymarket A3 that re-engines the overnight service from St Pancras arrives in Carlisle with the 17.20

Boswells where they change footplates with the 22.05 Class C from Dundee West. The latter does not leave Haymarket goods until 00.30 and is booked to be worked by the Carlisle A3 Pacific that arrived in Edinburgh with the Thames-Forth a short while ago.

Having to remember where trains have crew relief is not the only operating variable that has to be watched since some of the class C trains are booked to take banking assistance over Falahill and Whitrope whilst others are

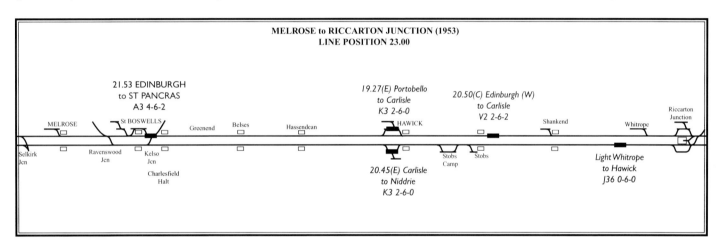

MELROSE to RICCARTON JUNCTION (1953)
LINE POSITION 23.00

- with parcels vans for Carlisle, Sheffield and Bristol and fish vans for Leicester, Nottingham, Birmingham, Sheffield, Leeds, Bradford, Liverpool, Manchester, Wigan and Carlisle.

A pair of passenger vehicles is included in the formation and the service is advertised as far as Hawick although the train continues complete to Carlisle. The non-passenger vehicles go forward from Carlisle in the 03.40 Derby Parcels.

The engine booked for the service is in the second part of its diagram; the first being the 08.30 Glasgow (Queen St) to Kings Cross between Edinburgh and Newcastle, returning

stopping train from Newcastle and is at the moment being prepared on Canal loco.

Maintaining an interested eye on 16 up sleeper, one ensures that the 19.27 Portobello - Carlisle goods has cleared the main line at Hawick where it will sit until the 22.15 Postal has passed. The train the 19.27 changes footplates with, the 20.45 Carlisle to Niddrie, is standing in the down side and will continue forward in a quarter of an hour.

While the majority of changeovers take place at Hawick, the 22.00 Carlisle to Edinburgh - which has just departed from Newcastleton - is an odd-man out since its Canal crew work to St

not. As a general rule down trains from Carlisle do not - in theory - require assistance whilst some of those from Edinburgh take a banker at Hardengreen. In practice the train load is the best guide although the weather is an important factor and it is never a good idea to assume that your banking engines are fully programmed for the next few hours. The final decision is made by the driver and it is not always easy to anticipate their intentions - the rule is always to keep an engine up your sleeve and it is astonishing how a sudden spell of rain can denude Hardengreen and Hawick of their engines!

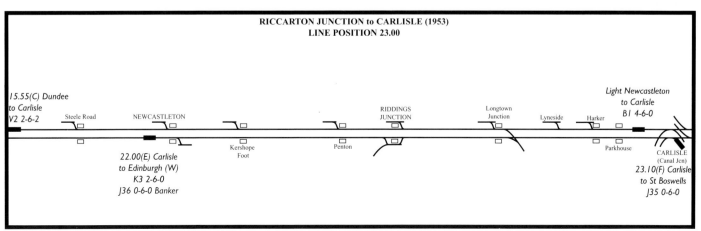

RICCARTON JUNCTION to CARLISLE (1953)
LINE POSITION 23.00

THE KELSO BRANCH

Hawick loco in 1955 with one of the 4-4-2 tanks booked to work the St Boswells - Berwick service. (W.S.Sellar)

The fact that the Waverley route passed through one of the most sparsely populated parts of the Kingdom did not prevent the main line spawning a number of cross-country lines that, if anything, served an even more remote part of the country.

Amongst these was the Kelso branch which, in unity with the North Eastern Railway, ran the thirty-five miles more or less due east to Tweedmouth, the most northerly station on the North Eastern main line. (Surprisingly, given the nature of the country, the Tweedmouth was paralleled by another eat-west line which ran from St Boswells to Reston, eleven miles north of Berwick. During the 1930's it was quite a simple matter to travel from St Boswells to Berwick by one route and return by the other but in 1948 the section between Duns and Greenlaw was washed away by flooding and the through service was never resumed).

Traffic on the Kelso line was shared between St Boswells and Tweedmouth sheds, the former using a C15 4-4-2T and a J36 0-6-0 from Hawick while the NER employed a G5 0-4-4T and a J39 0-6-0 for their workings

although in many cases the (not infrequent) unavailability of the booked engine at both ends of the line could result in some strange sights thanks to the line being able to take engine of the size of B1 4-6-0's and K3 2-6-0's.

The Working Timetable endorsed with the type of engines booked to each service is shown below. Through services to and from Berwick reversed at Tweedmouth with the engine running round the train.

The extended wait at Kelso by the through trains reflected the fact that historically trains from both Berwick and St Boswells had terminated there.

ST BOSWELLS - KELSO - COLDSTREAM - TWEEDMOUTH (BERWICK) : 1953

m.ch	Train From Class Engine	Pass C15	Pass C15	K J35	Pass G5	K J35	Pass G5	K J39	K J39	Pass C15	K J35	K J35	K J35	Pass C15	Pass C15	K J39	Pass G5
0.00	**St BOSWELLS**	06.22		06.45	08.33					11.38	13.30			16.05		16.55	19.15
3.01	Maxton		06/53	08.39							13.40	13.58		16.11		17/05	
5.43	Rutherford	06.32			08.44					11.48		14/10		16.16			19.25
8.48	Roxburgh Junction.			07.15	08.50					11.53		14.20		16.21		17.25	19.30
8.48	Roxburgh Junction.	06/36		07.50	08.51					11.54		14.44	16.05	16.23		17.35	19.31
9.10	Helton																
11.46	**KELSO**	06.41		08.00	08.56					11.59		14.54		16.28		17.45	19.36
11.46	**KELSO**		07.35			09.00	09.30	10.45							16.40	18.30	19.50
13.68	Sprouston		07.40				09.35	10.55	11.05						16.45		19.55
16.12	Carham		07.45				09.40		11.10						16.50		20.00
18.34	Sunilaws		07.50				09.45								16.55		20.05
21.38	**COLDSTREAM**		07.57				09.52		11.35						17.02	18.50	20.12
21.38	**COLDSTREAM**		08.00				09.59		12.30						17.05	19.30	20.15
24.31	Twizell		08.06				10.00								17.11		20.21
27.21	Norham		08.12				10.06								17.17		20.27
29.64	Velvet Hall		08.19				10.13								17.24		20.34
33.74	**TWEEEDMOUTH**		08.26				10.20		13.35						17.31	20.01	20.41
33.74	**TWEEEDMOUTH**		08.32				10.25								17.37		20.47
35.06	**BERWICK**		08.35				10.28								17.40		20.50
	Destination				J'burgh						J'burgh						

m.ch	Train From Class Engine	Pass G5	K J35	K J39	K J39	K J39	K J39	K J39	K J39	Pass C15	K J35 (12.30 Jedburgh)	K J35 (12.30 Jedburgh)	Pass C15	H J39	K J35	Pass G5 (17.15 Jedburgh)	K J35	Pass C15
0.00	**BERWICK**	06.30								09.20						15.28		18.40
1.12	**TWEEEDMOUTH**	06.33								09.23						15.31		18.43
1.12	**TWEEEDMOUTH**	06.40		07.30						09.28				13.50		15.38		18.50
5.22	Velvet Hall	06.47		07.45	07.52					09.35						15.45		18.57
7,65	Norham	06.52			08.02	08.15				09.40						15.50		19.02
10.55	Twizell	06.57				08.22	08.28			09.45						15.55		19.07
13.48	**COLDSTREAM**	07.04					08.40			09.52						16.02		19.14
13.48	**COLDSTREAM**	07.07					09.00			09.54				14/19		16.03		19.17
16.53	Sunilaws	07.13					09.10	09.25		10.00						16.09		19.23
18.74	Carham	07.18						09.35	09.40	10.05						16.14		19.28
21.18	Sprouston	07.23								10.10						16.19		19.33
23.40	**KELSO**	07.28							09.55	10.15					14.40	16.24		19.38
23.40	**KELSO**	07.43	08.30							10.31		14.21	15.00		15.40	16.31		19.46
25.76	Helton																	
26.38	Roxburgh Junction.	07.49	08.40							10.37	13.10		14.27		15.50	16.37	17.45	19.52
26.38	Roxburgh Junction.	07.50								10.38	13.20		14.29	15/10		16.39	18.10	19.53
29.43	Rutherford	07.57								10.45	13.30	13.35	14.35			16.45		20.05
32.05	Maxton									10.50						16.50		
35.06	**St BOSWELLS**	08.07								10.56	13.55	14.45	15.39			16.56	18.40	20.15
	Destination																	

The Border Counties line was absorbed by the North British Railway in 1860 as a sign of the Company's determination to reach Newcastle independently of the East Coast route via Berwick; an aim that was only indirectly reached since running powers had to be exercised over the 22 miles between Border Counties Junction, Hexham, and Newcastle.

The return on the investment was to have been the receipts from the movement of livestock and textiles from the Hawick area to the Tyneside conurbation and no doubt the volume of goods traffic met the costs of movement until road haulage started to abstract the railway's more valuable traffic.

Where exactly the North British expected its passenger traffic to materialise from is a matter for speculation. No-one but an enthusiast with time on his hands and money in his pocket would think of travelling from Edinburgh to Newcastle via any route other than Berwick whilst originating traffic was decidedly thin south of Falahill. On the other hand the line did a good trade in Sunday excursions: a typical July Sabbath in 1949, for example, would see a North Shields to Galashiels passing a Hawick to Tynemouth train for a total of eighteen packed corridor coaches.

As with numerous other rural lines, longevity was assured firstly by a world war and then by a national railway management that took nearly twenty years to decide whether it operated as a public service or as a commercial undertaking. During this interregnum, business as normal was the dictum of the Border Counties whose 1952 timetable was not vastly different from that of forty years earlier.

Three passenger workings operated to a pattern that required a Hawick D30 4-4-0 to remain overnight at Blaydon whilst a J36 0-6-0 made a return trip from Riccarton Junction to Hexham and back, making an interminable number of calls to set down empties and clear goods traffic.

Had the line remained under the aegis of the North British, it might have lasted into the 1960's but most of the route had been handed to the North Eastern in 1948 and they had little time for any line that lacked either a colliery or a steelworks. The Morpeth - Reedsmouth branch closed in September 1952 and it came as no great shock when the main line followed in October 1956.

D30 4-4-0 62425 'Ellangowan' on Hawick loco in September 1955. This engine was a regular performer on the two-day diagram that covered the Border Counties services. (W.S.Sellar)

RICCARTON JUNCTION - REEDSMOUTH JUNCTION - HEXHAM (1953)

Riccarton Junction to Hexham

m.ch / Station	06.15 Hawick Pass D30	07.20 R.Jcn K J36	Pass D30	K J39	Pass G5	16.32 Hawick Pass D30
0.00 **RICCARTON JUNCTION**	06.47	07.20	10.22			17.03
2.46 Saughtree		07.30 / 07.35				
5.52 Deadwater	06.55	07.45 / 07.50	10.32			17.13
8.18 Kiedler Forest	07.03	07.55 / 08.00	10.38			17.19
10.10 Lewiefield Halt	07.08		10.43			17.24
11.50 Plashetts	07.11	08.10 / 08.15	10.48			17.28
16.70 Falstone	07.20	08.30 / 08.35	10.56			17.36
20.15 Thorneyburn	07.27					17.43
21.40 Tarset	07.31	08.50 / 08.55	11.05			17.48
25.06 Bellingham	07.38	09.05 / 09.10	11.12	16.05		17.55
26.65 **REEDSMOUTH JCN**	07.42		11.16	16.09		17.59
26.65 **REEDSMOUTH JCN**	07.48	09/15	11.19	16.15		18.10
30.56 Wark	07.57	09.25 / 09.30	11.28			18.19
33.55 Barkus Siding		09.40 / 09.45				
34.38 Barrasford	08.04	09.50 / 09.55	11.35			18.26
35.54 Chollerton	08.08	10.00 / 10.05	11.39			18.30
36.30 Cocklaw Siding		10.10 / 10.15				
37.02 Humshaugh	08.13	10.20 / 10.25	11.43			18.34
38.67 Wall	08.18	10.30 / 10.35	11.47		14.30	18.38
40.19 Acomb Sidings						
40.71 Border Counties Jcn	08/22		11/51			18/42
41.78 **HEXHAM**	08.25	10.40	11.59		14.45	18.45
Destination	Ncle		Ncle	Canal	Scotsgap	Ncle

Hexham to Riccarton Junction

m.ch / Station	05.50 Ncle Pass D30	11.00 Hexham K J36	11.20 Ncle Pass D30	10.50 Canal J39	16.30 Ncle Pass D30
0.00 **HEXHAM**	06.51	11.00	12.07		17.15
1.07 Border Counties Jcn	06/53	11/03	12/10	12.52	17/18
1.59 Acomb Sidings		11.05		13.00	
3.11 Wall	06.59	11.15 / 11.20	12.15	14.05	17.23
4.76 Humshaugh	07.04	11.25 / 11.30	12.20	14.10	17.28
5.48 Cocklaw Siding					
6.24 Chollerton	07.09	11.35 / 11.40	12.24		17.32
7.40 Barrasford	07.13	11.45 / 11.50	12.28		17.36
8.13 Barkus Siding					
11.22 Wark	07.22	12.00 / 12.05	12.36		17.44
15.13 **REEDSMOUTH JCN**	07.30		12.44		17.52
15.13 **REEDSMOUTH JCN**	07.46	12/15	12.48	15.05	18.01
16.72 Bellingham	07.51	12.20 / 12.25	12.53	15.09	18.07
20.38 Tarset	07.58	12.35 / 12.40	13.00		18.13
21.63 Thorneyburn	08.02				18.17
25.08 Falstone	08.10	12.55	13.10		18.25
30.28 Plashetts	08.20	13.30 / 13.35	13.20		18.35
31.68 Lewiefield Halt	08.26		13.25		18.40
33.60 Kiedler Forest	08.34	13.45 / 13.50	13.32		18.47
36.26 Deadwater	08.40	13.55 / 14.00	13.38		
39.32 Saughtree		14.05 / 14.10			
41.78 **RICCARTON JUNCTION**	08.50	14.15	13.49		19.02
Destination	Hawick		Hawick		Hawick

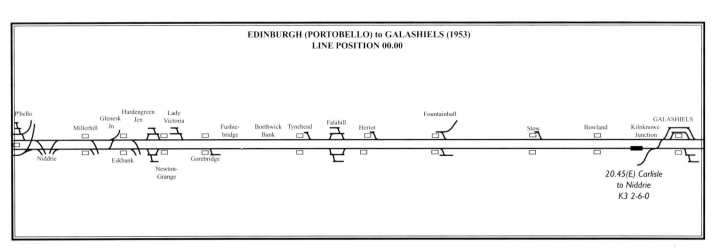

EDINBURGH (PORTOBELLO) to GALASHIELS (1953)
LINE POSITION 00.00

P'bello — Millerhill — Niddrie — Glenesk Jn — Eskbank — Hardengreen Jcn — Newton-Grange — Lady Victoria — Gorebridge — Fushie-bridge — Borthwick Bank — Tynehead — Falahill — Heriot — Fountainhall — Stow — Bowland — Kilnknowe Junction — GALASHIELS

20.45(E) Carlisle
to Niddrie
K3 2-6-0

CONTROLLER'S LOG: Galashiels: *"617 goods down at 56."*
Newcastleton: *"London up at 56."*
Stobs: *"529 goods at 58."*
Melrose: *"Hawick goods up at 59."*
Controller: *"St Boswells? Falahill goods next up to you in five minutes. 64539, 45 on with 28 to detach at you. Remainder for Hawick."*
Newcastleton: *"Boswells' goods down at 59."*
Hawick: *"Mail away at midnight."*
Canal: *"528 ready to leave. Engine 60090, Canal men and guard, Class E 45 equal 45 to the engine?"*
Controller: *"60840. 618, two-fifteen Meadows. There should be a set of spare men to turn it. The men who've brought it in take back 767 at one-thirty."*
Canal: *"Shall I send it to the loco for an hour? Get it out of the way."*
Controller: *"Yes."*
Hawick: *"Class E down main to Yard at seven. Is this a changeover?"*
Controller: *"No. They work through to St Boswells and changeover with 625 up."*
Controller: *"Hawick? Falahill goods next up to you. Seventeen on; engine to loco."*
Hawick: *"OK. Where's the Carlisle goods?"*
Controller: *"Steele Road."*
Canal Insp: *"The Upperby trip has brought in five vans for Melrose which they didn't tell me about. They should have been here yesterday for 3 down."*
Controller: *"Can you make room for them on the two-fifteen Meadows, 618 down?"*
Canal Jcn: *"London up at twenty-two."*
Canal Insp: *"I can get them on 618, yes."*

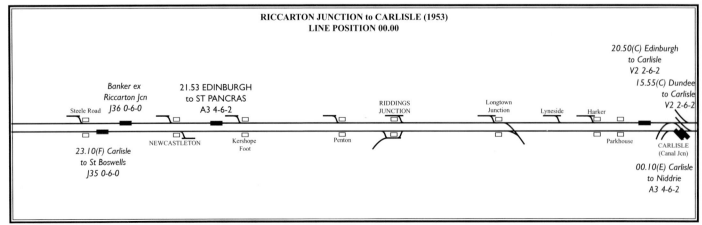

MELROSE to RICCARTON JUNCTION (1953)
LINE POSITION 00.00

19.27(E) Portobello
to Carlisle
K3 2-6-0

22.15 EDINBURGH
to CARLISLE
A4 4-6-2

23.15(H) Falahill
to Hawick
J37 0-6-0

MELROSE — Selkirk Jcn — St BOSWELLS — Ravenswood Jcn — Kelso Jcn — Charlesfield Halt — Greenend — Belses — Hassendean — HAWICK — Stobs Camp — Stobs — Shankend — Whitrope — Riccarton Junction

22.00(E) Carlisle
to Edinburgh (W)
K3 2-6-0

Niddrie."*
Controller: *"Did the driver say anything about needing a banker?"*
Carlisle: *"Didn't mention it."*
Newcastleton: *"Banker back at 01."*
Hawick: *"Can I let 558 goods onto the up?"*
Controller: *"Pull off."*
Hawick: *"558 away at five then."*
Niddrie Insp. *"What's on its way for me?"*
Controller: *"617 at Bowland and 528 just leaving Carlisle. Have you been given the loadings?"*
Niddrie Insp: *"Yes."*
Canal: *"557 arrived at six. What's happening*
Canal Jcn: *"528 down at ten."*
Riddings Jcn : *"London Passenger up at ten."*
St Boswells: *"Falahill goods in at ten."*
Controller: *"Canal Yard? 558 goods. 61882. 45=50 including 10 Gresty Lane, 12 Edge Hill, 5 Cheshire Lines. Right time from Hawick."*
Longtown Jcn: *"London up at thirteen."*
Newcastleton: *"The Banker driver is asking what his next job is?"*
Controller: *"528 down. Will be at you in half-an-hour."*
Stow: *"617 goods down at fifteen."*
St Boswells: *"Hawick goods away at eighteen. 64539; seventeen on for Hawick."*
Controller: *"Put them on the brake to come off at Hawick."*
Whitrope: *"243 up at twenty-six"*
Controller: *"Hawick? The two-fifteen Carlisle will have five Melrose on the brake for 558 bonus which'll want to be taken off by the pilot while the crew are changing over."*
Hawick: *"558 doesn't call at Melrose."*
Controller: *"I know that. 558 can take them to St Boswells for the midday trip to Melrose."*
Hawick: *"I'll get the guard of 558 to knock them off on the way."*
Controller: *"As long as he's prepared to position them and won't take all day about it."*

RICCARTON JUNCTION to CARLISLE (1953)
LINE POSITION 00.00

20.50(C) Edinburgh
to Carlisle
V2 2-6-2

15.55(C) Dundee
to Carlisle
V2 2-6-2

Banker ex
Riccarton Jcn
J36 0-6-0

21.53 EDINBURGH
to ST PANCRAS
A3 4-6-2

Steele Road — NEWCASTLETON — Kershope Foot — Penton — RIDDINGS JUNCTION — Longtown Junction — Lyneside — Harker — Parkhouse — CARLISLE (Canal Jcn)

23.10(F) Carlisle
to St Boswells
J35 0-6-0

00.10(E) Carlisle
to Niddrie
A3 4-6-2

D30 4-4-0 62432 'Quentin Durward' leaves Hawick with the 12.20 (Saturdays Only) Hawick to Carlisle on 9th September 1950 and gets to grips with the initial 1 in 75 of Whitrope bank.

Carlisle Canal was transferred to the London Midland in 1958 and although it made little difference to the allocation initially, any shortfall in availability had to be made good from the LM and thus the chances of foreign engines appearing on Waverley route trains increased considerably.   Problems with the Canal A3 allocation in December 1961 was probably the reason that Britannia 70016 'Ariel' was found on the 09.20 Carlisle - Edinburgh instead of the usual Carlisle A3 Pacific. (W.S.Sellar)

Released from Kittybrewster by the dieselisation of the Great North of Scotland, a handful of BR Standard 4MT 2-6-4T's gravitated south for the final years of steam operation and a small number could be found at Hawick. One of their number was 80113 which is seen at Whitrope summit in December 1961 with the 12.28 (SO) Hawick - Carlisle stopping train. (W.S.Sellar)

The 2nd of December 1961 seems to have been a day when Edinburgh had a glut of Pacifics for instead of the usual K3 2-6-0, A2 Pacific 60529 'Pearl Diver' was sent out to work the 08.15 Niddrie to Carlisle which is seen coasting through Riccarton Junction. (W.S.Sellar)

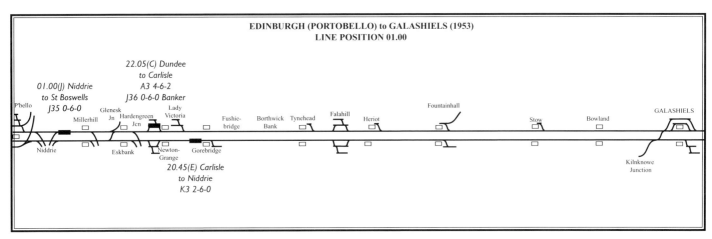

EDINBURGH (PORTOBELLO) to GALASHIELS (1953)
LINE POSITION 01.00

CONTROLLERS LOG: For historic reasons the Waverley route has a name for being something of an economic millstone; a reputation derived from the fact that the public timetable has never amounted to more than a pair of pages. The heavy tonnage of goods traffic that brings the money in is, alas, hidden from public gaze.

For many years the line had a source of unearned income which resulted from an arrangement reached with the Midland Railway who guaranteed the North British a minimum level of through bookings from London. Since this level was never reached, the North British found itself the grateful recipient of funds

something to shed too many tears over.

Goods trains from both ends of the operating spectrum are present with a pair of class C expresses arriving on the section at Carlisle and Hardengreen respectively whilst at the other end of the scale a J37 0-6-0 backs the 23.15 class H from Falahill into Hawick Yard. This train collects coal traffic for Galashiels, St Boswells and Hawick that has been worked into Falahill by unscheduled trip workings from Hardengreen.

On the other side of Hawick yard the 22.00 Carlisle to Portobello sets down and picks up traffic and one has to remind oneself that this is one of the few trains that does not change crews

train) and the other being the 01.10 Carlisle - Dundee the engine of which will return south with the up Thames-Forth.

As usual K3 2-6-0's and A3 Pacifics dominate the through goods work but there are a handful of mainline turns that use smaller and older engines; one such being the Falahill trip which has just arrived in Hawick. Another is the 23.10 Carlisle - St Boswells goods which has just started the descent of Whitrope. The engine used for this service is a St Boswells' J36 0-6-0, outbased from Hawick. After shunting its train, the 0-6-0 will be used to work the 06.45 goods from St Boswells to Kelso and Jedburgh.

This is not the only engine to be out-based

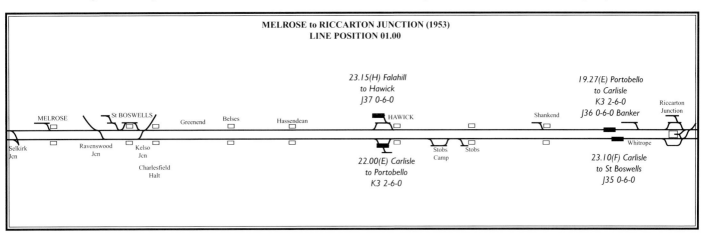

MELROSE to RICCARTON JUNCTION (1953)
LINE POSITION 01.00

for providing a train service that few people seemed to want.

Anyone looking at the train board would realise that passenger traffic is not the mainstay of the route since the nearest thing to a passenger train in the 100-mile section is the up postal which does not convey passengers south of Hawick.

Goods traffic is plentiful and since it can move without having to run for cover every few miles, the absence of passenger traffic is not

at Hawick but changes instead at St Boswells with the 22.05 Dundee (West) to Carlisle.

The latter, which is just taking banking assistance at Hardengreen, is a Pacific working and returns the Carlisle engine that brought down the 09.15 St Pancras - Edinburgh.

Towards the Southern end of the district, two more A3 Pacifics can be seen on goods work: one being the 00.10 from Carlisle (the return working of the engine that went south with the 14.33 Edinburgh - Carlisle stopping

at St Boswells and the shed there normally has an allocation of three J36 0-6-0's (for the 04.50 to Galashiels, the 06.45 to Kelso and the 13.30 to Kelso) and a C15 4-4-2T. The latter shares the Berwick-upon-Tweed workings with a Tweedmouth G5 0-4-4T; the C15 working the 06.22 and 16.05 services from St Boswells to Berwick with an intermediate (11.38) trip to Kelso. When a C15 is not available almost anything, including B1 and K3 engines, is used as a substitute.

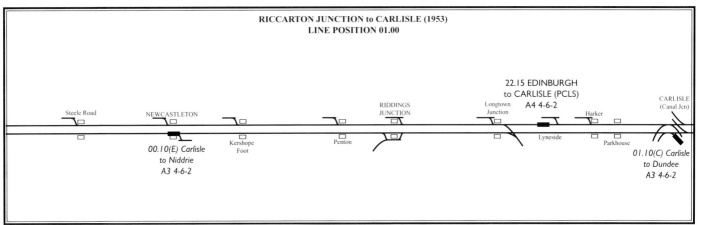

RICCARTON JUNCTION to CARLISLE (1953)
LINE POSITION 01.00

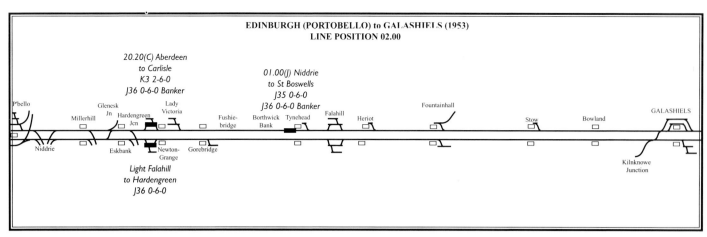

EDINBURGH (PORTOBELLO) to GALASHIELS (1953)
LINE POSITION 02.00

CONTROLLER'S LOG: The role of pregrouping engines does not finish with the 23.10 Carlisle - St Boswells goods and while that rattles away the last few miles of its diagram, another J36 0-6-0 appears from the Edinburgh direction with the 01.00 Niddrie to St Boswells. Upon arrival the engine will pick up any Galashiels traffic left in St Boswells by the 23.10 ex Carlisle and then continue with local trips on the Greenlaw and Melrose lines until finishing duty in the early afternoon. In the midst of such musings arrangements have to be made with Falahill to have the J36 and

goods from Kings Cross which should be a few south of Berwick-upon-Tweed. A Dundee portion will be transferred from the East Coast train to the 01.10 whilst the latter is changing engines.

The second class C, the 01.30 from Carlisle, conveys only traffic for Perth and Highland Railway destinations but also changes engine at Niddrie. The twenty minute interval between the two services is held throughout from Carlisle to Edinburgh and in spite of the activities at Niddrie, the separation between the pair by the time they part company at Inverkeithing is only

and will have to be cleared out of the way of the approaching expresses both of which call at Hawick. Since the 00.10 is in no hurry - it changes over with the 20.20 ex Aberdeen which is only at Hardengreen - it can sit in the loop at Stobs for an hour and come out when things have quietened down.

The 20.20 ex Aberdeen is preceded by another class C, the 22.05 Dundee West to Carlisle, which has a completely clear run to Carlisle. The only stop it will make will be at St Boswells to change crews with the 22.00 from Carlisle and it should climb Whitrope

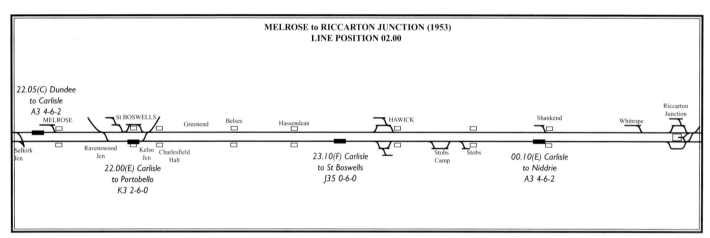

MELROSE to RICCARTON JUNCTION (1953)
LINE POSITION 02.00

its train shunted for the Aberdeen - Carlisle express goods which is attaching a banker at Hardengreen.

At the English end of the line two class C express goods - the return workings of the Edinburgh men who worked through to Carlisle - are running almost block and block and are booked to climb to Whitrope without the aid of a banker.

The leading train - the 01.10 ex Canal - calls for some liaison with the East Coast Controller since it has to connect at Niddrie with the 15.05

seventeen minutes.

The urgency with which both trains are worked is impressive and the 182-minute timing from Canal to Niddrie - which includes an eleven minute pause at Hawick - is only eighteen minutes slower than the Carlisle - Edinburgh booking of the down St Pancras sleeper.

The first of the class C trains will be at Hawick in half an hour and the 00.10 from Canal - a plodding unfitted class E in spite of its Pacific - is in danger of becoming an obstacle

bank unassisted. This Dundee service is another instance of ex-Caledonian traffic being routed over the North British system in order to free a path and set of men for Glasgow traffic on the line over Beattock.

The supply of Pacifics and V2's does not quite stretch to all the principal services and although being in the first rank of express goods workings, the 20.20 Aberdeen - Carlisle has to make do with a K3 2-6-0. The use of a Pacific on the much slower 00.10 Carlisle to Niddrie is simply a quirk of diagramming.

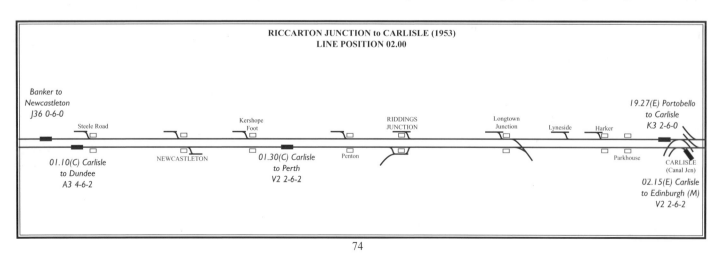

RICCARTON JUNCTION to CARLISLE (1953)
LINE POSITION 02.00

On 2nd December 1961 the photographer stationed himself in an exposed position by Shankend viaduct on a very cold day in the expectation of capturing a Pacific being worked hard by its booked A3 Pacific on the 1 in 81 climb to Whitrope. When the train turned up over Shankend viaduct with one of the new D53xx Type 2 diesel-electrics, his thoughts are better imagined than spelled out. (W.S.Sellar)

The engine for the 10.05 Edinburgh - St Pancras 'Thames-Forth Express' was a Carlisle A3 which worked down on the 01.10 Carlisle - Niddrie express goods before working the 08.34 Corstorphine - Edinburgh which formed the St Pancras service. Something, however, went wrong on the 26th July 1952 since the booked engine failed to get to the Waverley by 10.05 and V2 60934 of York - seen approaching Carlisle - had to be substituted. Judging by the level of coal in the tender and the general state of the engine, it seems that the substitution was made at rather short notice.

J36 0-6-0 65312 stands under the imposing bulk of Canal Junction whilst running light on the Edinburgh main line from Canal loco to Canal Yard. The Silloth branch is to the immediate left of the signalbox while the two lines closest to the camera are shunting necks for Canal Yard which lies to the right of the photographer. The divergence of the lines to Carlisle station and the goods line to Upperby via Dalston Junction lie just out of sight to the right of the camera. Canal loco is situated about half a mile behind Canal Junction signalbox. (W.S.Sellar)

Most trip working was performed by N15 0-6-2T or 3F 0-6-0T's but an excess of traffic (or a shortage of pilots) has obliged Canal shed to turn out K3 2-6-0 61936 to work Target 76 with a train of Midland traffic from Canal Yard to Durran Hill South. Rather unusually the train has been directed to run via Caldew Junction, where it is seen above, as opposed to the more normal route via Dalston Road. The reason for the diversion is probably congestion on the direct line. The engine has a full tender of coal and this suggests that it will be required for a turn to Niddrie when it returns to Canal.

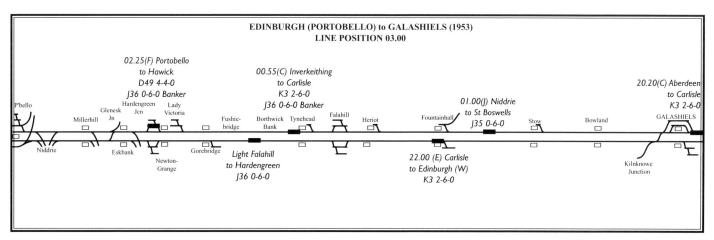

EDINBURGH (PORTOBELLO) to GALASHIELS (1953)
LINE POSITION 03.00

02.25(F) Portobello to Hawick
D49 4-4-0
J36 0-6-0 Banker

00.55(C) Inverkeithing to Carlisle
K3 2-6-0
J36 0-6-0 Banker

01.00(J) Niddrie to St Boswells
J35 0-6-0

20.20(C) Aberdeen to Carlisle
K3 2-6-0

Light Falahill to Hardengreen
J36 0-6-0

22.00 (E) Carlisle to Edinburgh (W)
K3 2-6-0

CONTROLLER'S LOG: The 22 Scottish members of the D49 4-4-0 are only occasional visitors to the Waverley route and although a pair are allocated to Carlisle, they are normally confined to the southern end of the line.

Most of their workings at the Northern end of the line have been taken over in recent years by B1 4-6-0's but the early riser can still catch sight of a D49 on a daily basis, one of the Haymarket engines being diagrammed to work the 02.25 Portobello to Hawick goods which can be seen waiting for its banker at Hardengreen Junction. A class F goods is rather an unusual assignment for a 4-4-0 but

allocating engines to trains and while this may be a straightforward task at St Margaret's and Haymarket, it can be far from simple at outstations such as St Boswells and Galashiels.

The position at Riccarton Junction illustrates the problem well. The small shed has to provide a J36 for the day-shift banker (off shed at 05.00), a D30 4-4-0 for the 07.12 Carlisle passenger and another J36 for the 07.20 Reedsmouth goods. All three engines have been on the shed overnight whilst a fourth - a J36 0-6-0 - has been covering the night-shift banker. If a fault develops with one of the engines during the night - not an unknown

At this time of morning one tends to look rather anxiously at the phone, wondering who will be the first to call in with a tale of woe.

On the main line the progress of the northbound express goods trains is being monitored carefully. With the 23.10 from Carlisle safely inside at St Boswells, the 23.10 Carlisle to Dundee has a clear path for twenty miles ahead while the following Perth goods gets ready to leave Hawick after a brief stop - not unwelcome to its fireman - to exchange traffic. With these two expresses well on their way, the 00.10 Carlisle to Niddrie can be plucked out of the down loop at Stobs Camp

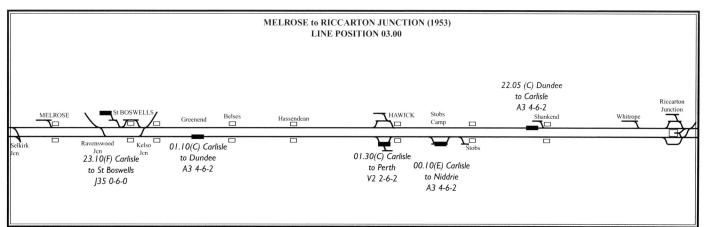

MELROSE to RICCARTON JUNCTION (1953)
LINE POSITION 03.00

22.05 (C) Dundee to Carlisle
A3 4-6-2

23.10(F) Carlisle to St Boswells
J35 0-6-0

01.10(C) Carlisle to Dundee
A3 4-6-2

01.30(C) Carlisle to Perth
V2 2-6-2

00.10(E) Carlisle to Niddrie
A3 4-6-2

the object is to get an engine in position for the 06.44 Hawick - Edinburgh passenger.

With only an hour's turn-round in Hawick, it is not a particularly brilliant piece of diagramming and it is as well to keep another engine up one's sleeve in case the Portobello goods runs late. The Haymarket men hand the 4-4-0 over to a local crew at Hawick and return to Edinburgh with the St Pancras sleeper.

Three in the morning is the time of day when sheds start 'setting their stalls out' for the coming day. Much of this consists of

occurrence - then the night shift banker will probably have to be substituted in spite of the fact that after eight hours work on Whitrope bank the smokebox may be up to the door in ash while the firebars will be closing up with clinker.

The shed will be one engine short which, out of an allocation that can be counted on the fingers of one hand, puts it in an uncomfortable position. The loss will have to be made good by Hawick which itself does not have an inexhaustible supply of engines.

and be allowed down to Hawick where it can change footplates with the 20.20 Aberdeen - Carlisle which passed Galashiels a few minutes ago.

It is interesting to note how much traffic far-off Aberdeen produces since the 20.20 is only one of two through services to Carlisle. A second train, also a class C express, leaves Craiginches at 22.25 and runs through to Carlisle (Upperby), conveying only LNW traffic. This is the only Waverley route goods not to terminate in Canal Yard.

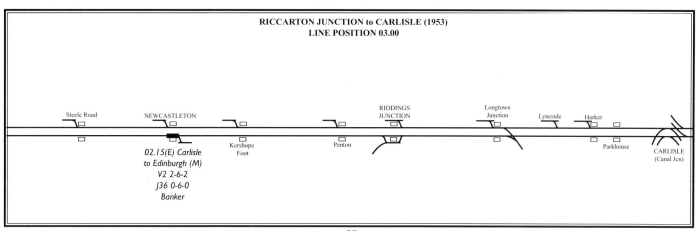

RICCARTON JUNCTION to CARLISLE (1953)
LINE POSITION 03.00

02.15(E) Carlisle to Edinburgh (M)
V2 2-6-2
J36 0-6-0 Banker

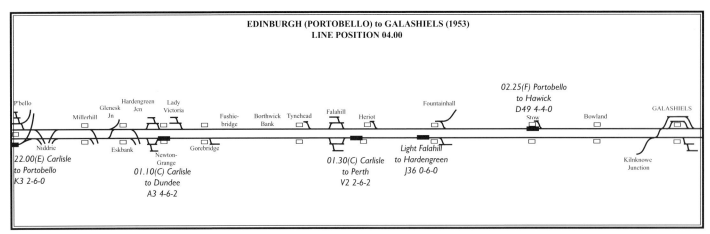

EDINBURGH (PORTOBELLO) to GALASHIELS (1953)
LINE POSITION 04.00

CONTROLLER'S LOG: The time arrives when a balance has to be struck between traffic on hand at each yard and the trains booked out in the early morning. The first part of this - the stocktaking - is a simple matter of speaking to each yard and obtaining the number of wagons for each destinations. Essentially this should do little more than confirm what you already know - a rough running tally having been kept during the night - but occasional confirmation by the man on the ground cannot be dispensed with. Once the stock has been obtained, it is then necessary to ensure that the train service will cope. Given the rural nature of the area, the number of morning goods services is higher than might be expected. St Boswells has three

Whilst discussing the loading of trains with the yards, an unspoken farewell is said to 529 down as its K3 2-6-0 drags it into Portobello yard. The reason for the acknowledgement is that this particular train has kept us company throughout the night shift, leaving Carlisle as we took duty at 22.00 and remaining as a measure of time ever since. Six hours for the 94-miles is a little excessive - an hour an a half longer than most class E trains - but seventy minutes was spent at Hawick attaching and detaching traffic with a further thirty at St Boswells.

The 00.10 from Carlisle - now passing Belses - is a similar companion and will be with us until the last few minutes of the shift. Such a romantic empathy with trains may sound a little

West Yard where they also change engines. In addition to this in an ambitious piece of scheduling, the Dundee train also takes forward a portion that arrives in the 15.05 from Kings Cross. The latter arrives in Niddrie West at 03.57 and is on its way again, in the Carlisle train, only sixty-one minutes later.

One of the differences between the fast freight on the East Coast main line and that of the Waverley route is that the former sees numerous express goods trains that run through from the point of origin - Kings Cross, Whitemoor, Dringhouses, Heaton, etc - while those of the latter all start from Carlisle and are made up from wagons that have arrived from one or other of the LMS constituents. There is

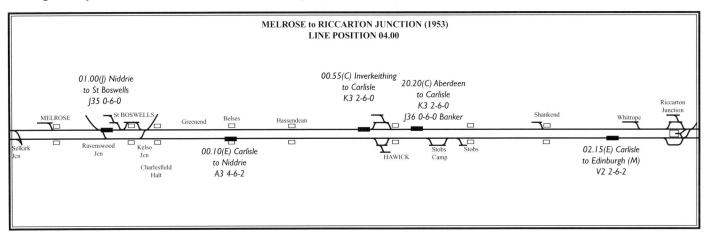

MELROSE to RICCARTON JUNCTION (1953)
LINE POSITION 04.00

services (04.50 to Galashiels, 06.10 to Greenlaw and 06.45 to Kelso), Galashiels, two (06.40 Selkirk and 09.26 Lauder) whilst Riccarton Junction and Galashiels have one apiece to Reedsmouth and Edinburgh respectively. The standard engine for most of these workings is the J36 0-6-0 - the Lauder branch is worked by a J67 0-6-0T - although with the problems alluded to earlier, strangers are often provided at short notice by Carlisle or St Margarets.

fanciful - as perhaps it is - but the moon that looks down on 528 shines also on us.

The Dundee and Perth express goods are getting very close to Edinburgh and a reminder to the Edinburgh controller of their approach will not go amiss since he will have to ensure that the replacement engines and relieving crews are in the right place when needed. Both trains come off the main line at Niddrie South Junction to set down and attach traffic in the

no goods equivalent to the Thames-Forth!

The southern end of the district is very quiet at the moment although with good reason since the pair of up Class C express goods in the vicinity of Hawick have to have the clearest run possible whilst in the down direction the 04.08 Carlisle - Edinburgh postal will soon be on its way and this train - one of the few to be booked to an A4 Pacific - has a priority equal to the overnight sleeper.

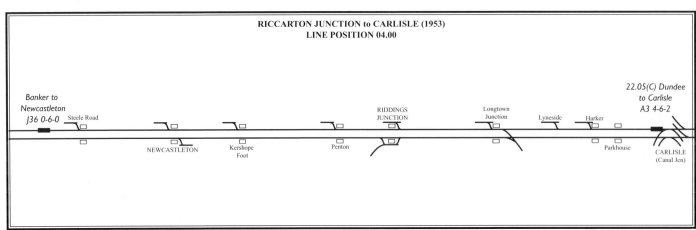

RICCARTON JUNCTION to CARLISLE (1953)
LINE POSITION 04.00

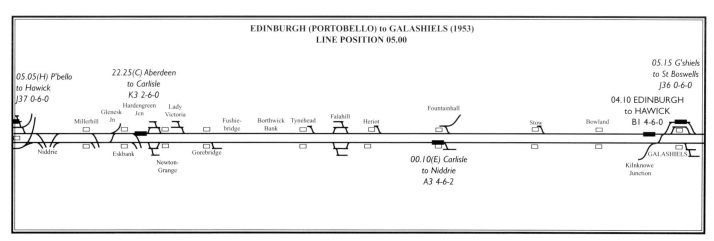

EDINBURGH (PORTOBELLO) to GALASHIELS (1953)
LINE POSITION 05.00

CONTROLLER'S LOG : The clerk drops a wire (telegram) onto the desk. *"From Train Control Derby. Train 185. Engine 45573 BG (Perth), BG (Glasgow St.E), BG,TK,TK,TK, CK, CK, SLC, BG (Edinburgh)."* In times gone the Midland trains used to convey (usually short-lived) through coaches to Perth, Inverness or Aberdeen and although the practice ceased years ago, Derby still maintains the habit of telegraphing the details of all through Anglo-Scottish trains. To the untrained eye the message - which gives details of the overnight

Newcastle turns up with a B1 4-6-0 or K1 2-6-0; its Pacific having failed or been commandeered for an East Coast service at Newcastle. When this happens the B1 or K1 is allocated to the 00.10 Canal to Niddrie Class E goods: a move which releases an A3 for the sleeper and gives the trainspotters of Edinburgh something to write home about.

An hour ahead of the sleeper - and just passing Whitrope summit - is the Carlisle - Edinburgh postal; the return working of the Waverley route's only A4 duty. Behind it the

had its change of crew at Hawick and should not stop again until reaching Meadows yard, Edinburgh. The Postal on the other hand calls at Hawick, St Boswells, Melrose and Galashiels and these stops should enable the 02.15 goods to keep ahead all the way to Edinburgh.

In the opposite direction a D49 4-4-0 pulls away from St Boswells with the Portobello - Hawick goods while a B1 4-6-0 approaches Galashiels with the Hawick News. This train has a very high priority and even a minute's delay will cause howls of protest from the

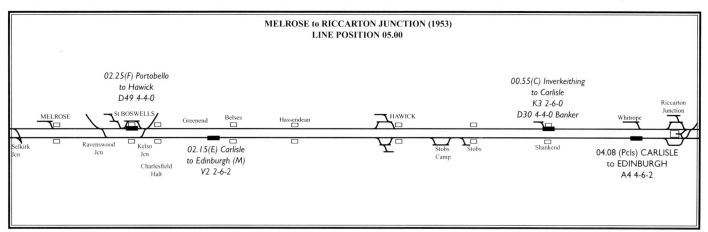

MELROSE to RICCARTON JUNCTION (1953)
LINE POSITION 05.00

express from St Pancras - casts more darkness than light since the engine will be replaced at Carlisle by an A3 Pacific whilst the leading pair of vehicles will be removed to go forward on the 21.15 St Pancras to St Enoch and the 22.52 Euston - Perth respectively.

The A3 Pacific in question has had a varied time since ringing off Haymarket shed twenty-four hours ago to work the 05.25 Haymarket to Canal class E goods - not the most appropriate task for an A3 - before continuing with the 14.00 Carlisle to Newcastle and the 17.20 Newcastle to Carlisle.

There are of course days when the 17.20 ex

K3-hauled 04.20 Canal to Portobello passes Kershope Foot, its progress being carefully watched to ensure it does not become an obstacle to the St Pancras sleeper. It has a single-engine load and should not therefore need a banking engine for the climb to Whitrope. If the driver decides otherwise the train can be shunted at Newcastleton until the sleeper has gone by. All being well, however, the 04.20 should keep going as far as Riccarton Junction before having to go inside.

The 02.15 Carlisle to Meadows, which is near Greenend, is similarly monitored in relation to the down Postal. The 02.15 has

Newspaper Association. A J36 0-6-0 and brakevan waits to follow for St Boswells where it will shunt and work the 06.10 goods to Greenlaw. Another 0-6-0, a J37, creeps over the boundary at Portobello and crosses the junction with the east coast route with a train for Hawick.

The shift approaches its end and in an hour or so the night shift will be abed and sleeping - one trusts - the sleep of the just while a colleague, who is now rising, will take control - literally - for an eight or twelve hour stretch of day time duty. It is always a busy job, sometimes exciting but never dull.

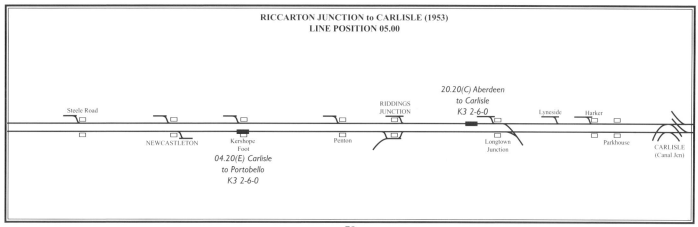

RICCARTON JUNCTION to CARLISLE (1953)
LINE POSITION 05.00

"Coaled for Leeds!" As usual Haymarket have turned out the Thames-Forth engine with enough coal to run to Leeds should the LMS 5XP 4-6-0 not be in place to take the train forward. 65 'Knight of Thistle' of Haymarket, seen entering Carlisle with the up Thames-Forth in 1947, was soon to become a rare sight north of the Border since it was transferred to Kings Cross in July 1950 and remained on the Great Northern until being withdrawn in June 1964.

Canal engines were not noted for their cleanliness and the shed's reputation in this respect is upheld by A3 60079 'Bayardo' as it arrives in Carlisle with the 10.05 Edinburgh - St Pancras in 1957 shortly after the service, formerly known as the 'Thames-Forth Express', had been rechristened 'The Waverley'. 60079 will be relieved by a Holbeck 5XP 4-6-0 and after turning will work back to Edinburgh with the corresponding down train, the 09.15 St Pancras to Edinburgh. One hopes that somewhere under the pile of dust in the tender, there might be some coal.